Ingo Bauernfeind

THE
CIVIL WAR
VOLUME 1

Copyright © 2013
Author/Publisher: Ingo Bauernfeind
Hingbergstrasse 86—88
45468 Mülheim an der Ruhr
Germany
www.ingobauernfeind.com

ISBN 978-3-9815984-0-7

ACKNOWLEDGEMENTS

Dr. Robert K. Sutton, Chief Historian, National Park Service
Eastern National
Dr. Alexandra Lord, Branch Chief, National Historic Landmarks Program, NPS
U.S. National Park Service (NPS)
U.S. Library of Congress
U.S. National Archives
U.S. Naval Historical Center
The Ultimate History Project
Nicole Laka

Layout: Nicole Laka, Hamburg, Germany
Cover design: Nicole Laka/ Anita Böning
3D conversion: Rehmbrand Medientechnik GmbH, Munich, Germany

Ingo Bauernfeind

THE
CIVIL WAR

VOLUME 1

PREFACE

BY ROBERT K. SUTTON, PH.D.,
CHIEF HISTORIAN OF THE NATIONAL PARK SERVICE

In 1838, Sir Charles Wheatstone described the phenomenon of stereopsis, by which human eyes transmit two separate images from different points of view to the brain, so that it perceives three dimensional depth. To demonstrate his concept, he later developed a stereoscope, which placed two mirrors on either end of a stand, with two slightly different images placed at angles in the center, producing 3D depth perception. Across the English Channel, at about the same time Wheatstone postulated stereopsis,

Early stereo image of Great Britain's Queen Victoria. Originally published by Underwood & Underwood, this image is now in the photo collection of the Library of Congress.

Victor'a, Queen and Empress from 1837 to 1901—England's most beloved and longest reigning Sovereign. Copyright 1901 by Underwood & Underwood.

two Frenchmen, Louis Daguerre and Joseph Nicéphore Niépce, were experimenting with creating photographic images, using a camera to produce pictures on metal plates. By 1839, Daguerre and Niépce's son had perfected the camera and process to produce daguerreotypes, creating permanent fixed images that could not be damaged by light, thus ushering in the birth of photography. Over the next decade-and-a-half, others further perfected the photographic processes, developing negative images, from which positive prints could be mass produced.

It didn't take long before photographers were producing 3D images with stereo cameras, to expose images side-by-side, simulating perspectives of right and left eyes. These cameras were not anything like modern-day digital cameras. A wet glass plate was inserted into each side of the stereo camera, then exposed by removing the lens caps for about twenty seconds. Once exposed, the plates were removed, immediately transferred to a portable darkroom, where they were

Civil War photographers.

Early stereoscope or stereo viewer (Image: Tangopaso).

rinsed and fixed with potassium cyanide as a permanent negative. The images were printed on cards, side-by-side, and viewed in 3D with stereoscopes.

Visitors to the Great London Exhibition in 1851 were able to see an image of Queen Victoria in stereo. Oliver Wendell Holmes, Sr., father of Civil War veteran and later Supreme Court Justice Oliver Wendell Holmes, Jr., created a streamlined stereoscope viewer that was inexpensive, and consisted of two prismatic lenses and a wooden stand to hold the stereo card. Many Civil War photographs produced by Mathew Brady and others, gave us vivid images of the carnage of war, of life in the camps, and of many soldiers, officers, and politicians of the day—produced in stereo. Many of us were introduced to 3D photography, seeing images of the Grand Canyon, Carlsbad Caverns, and Disney characters on the popular View-Master viewer. Ironically, the View-Master was introduced at the New York World's Fair in 1939, exactly 100 years after the birth of photography. 3D movies gained popularity in the 1950s, and continue to be shown in theaters and in venues such as Disney World and IMAX theaters. Even 3D televisions are now available.

Until recently, Civil War 3D images could be viewed with stereoscopes, but only the most hard-core Civil War enthusiasts wanted to bother with this old technology. Through modern technology, however, these historic photographs can be converted into 3D images that can be easily viewed with red-cyan glasses— just like in a movie theater. Side-by-side Civil War photographs are converted into anaglyphs, which place both on top of each other. The images are coded with red on one side and cyan (mixed green and blue) on the other. Through the red-cyan glasses, one side blocks out the cyan color, and the other the red, creating depth and thus the 3D image.

In his magnificent volume, Ingo Bauernfeind transports you back in time to the Civil War Era. You will feel like you are almost part of the council of war, presided over by General Ulysses S. Grant, just before the Battle of the Wilderness in 1864.

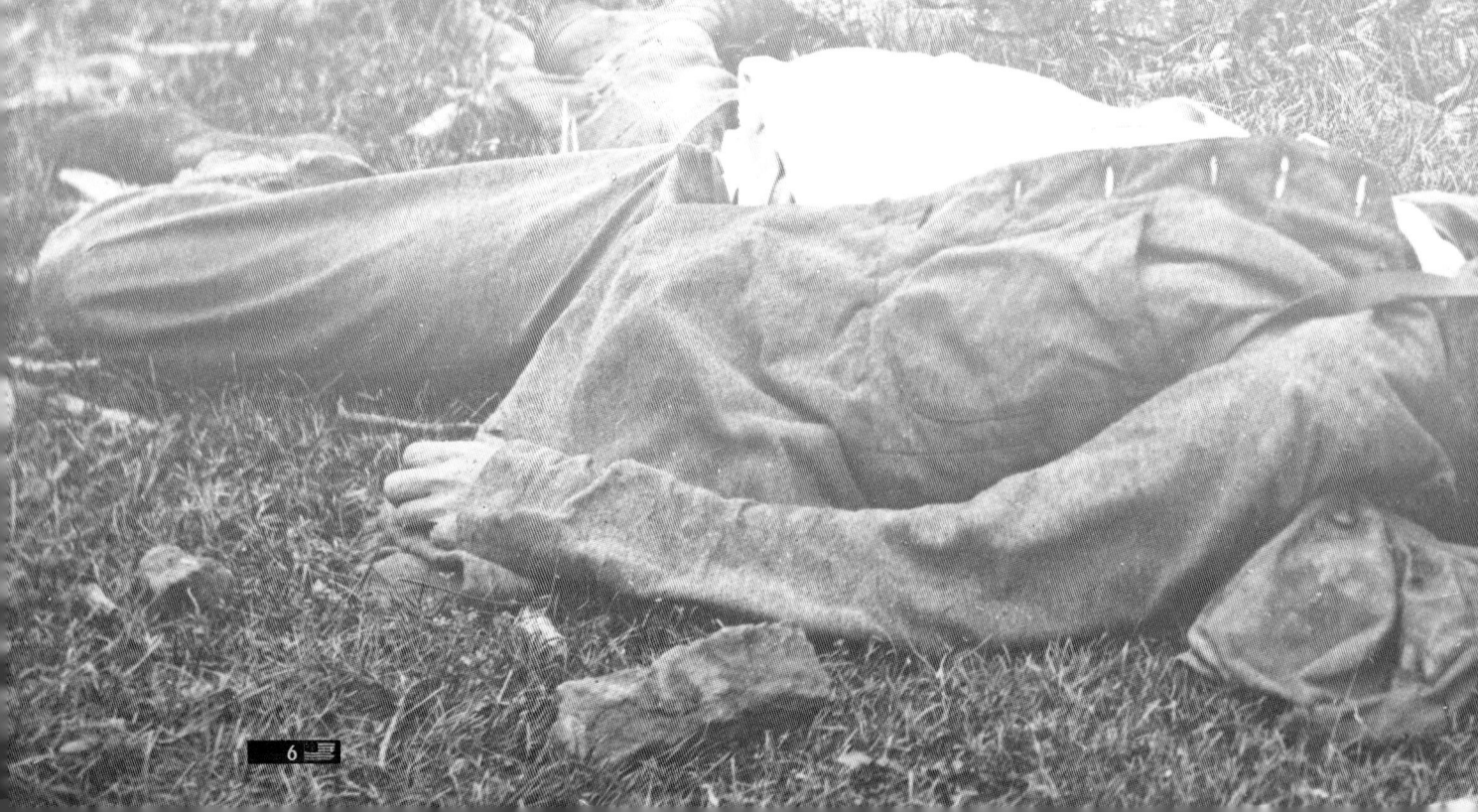

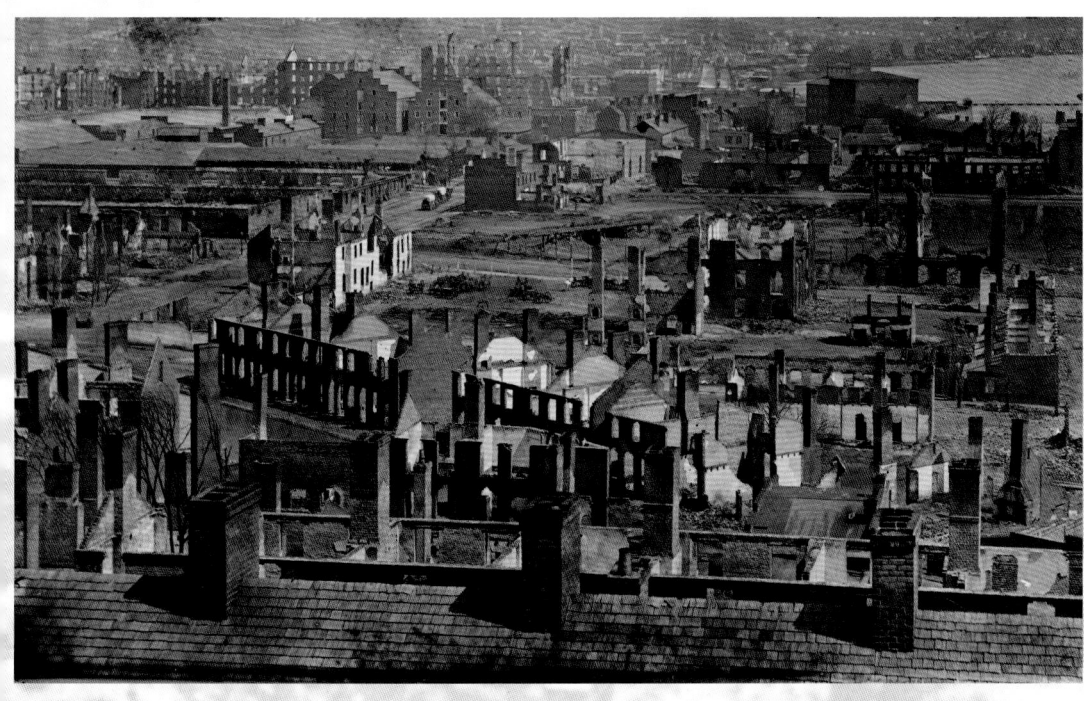

The ruins of Richmond, Virginia, 1865.

You can almost hear the groaning from the scenes of the Civil War field hospital. Modern inventions from the period—such as ironclad ships—come to life with 3D photography. As the war progressed, more and more images of African American soldiers were taken. In fact, you will see images of a slave pen captured by the Union in Alexandria, Virginia, as well as young African American men in their fighting uniforms (the contraband of war).

Nothing, however, is as poignant as the numerous 3D images of dead soldiers on the battlefields, or the legacy of the war—acres and acres of grave markers in Civil War cemeteries.

There is an old adage that "A picture is worth a thousand words." When you see the 3D images in this volume, you might want to change that to "A 3D image is worth two thousand words!"

INTRODUCTION
IMAGING THE FIRST MODERN WAR IN 3D

RIGHT The war left countless graves behind.

The American Civil War demonstrated for the first time how the technology of the emerging industrial age had transformed the nature of warfare. It was the first major conflict in which the train transported troops and material, thus turning railroad junctions, like Manassas Junction, Chattanooga, Atlanta, and Petersburg, into significant military objectives. The superiority of ironclad ships (such as the famed USS *Monitor*) to wooden vessels, revolutionized naval warfare. The use of the telegraph made instantaneous communication between generals possible. The Civil War saw the advent of armored trains, hand grenades, reconnaissance balloons, and early operational submarines: the Confederate Navy's *H.L. Hunley* was wholly functional—she even sank a Union ship before mysteriously sinking herself.

Innovations in weapons manufacturing resulted in new rifled muskets, with grooved barrels, firing recently developed Minié balls, that were easy to load, and with an accuracy up to 600 yards. With its superior accuracy at long distance, this firearm made the traditional lines of fire, in which soldiers stood and kneeled shoulder-to-shoulder, deadly

Confederate soldier posing with his rifle.

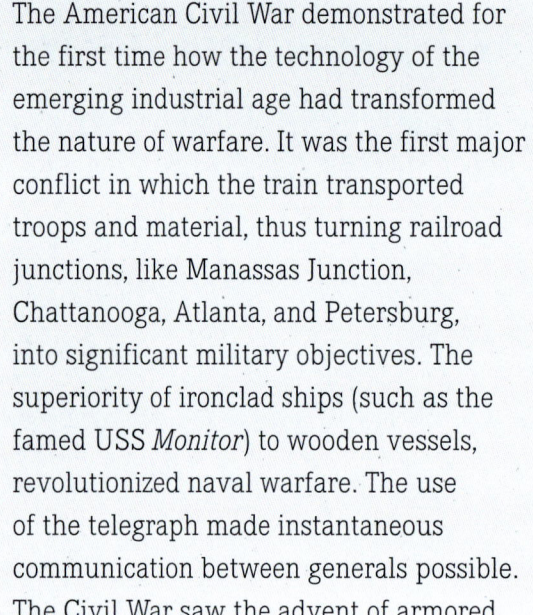

Confederate submarine
H.L. Hunley (Naval Historical Center Photo Collection).

at first and obsolete later. Strong fortifications and complex trenches became increasingly important, and gave the defending armies—mostly the Confederate troops—an enormous advantage over the attacking enemy. Improved weaponry made masonry forts—that could be reduced to rubble with relative ease—obsolete. They were replaced by earthwork fortifications.

Although true machine guns would not be invented for another two decades, the Gatling gun, a rotating bundle of gun barrels each firing in turn, was in use. It became the predecessor for modern machine guns. This rifle-and-trench warfare resulted in unbelievable casualties—Gettysburg alone saw over 50,000 dead, wounded, and missing. During the Civil War years, almost the same number of Americans lost their lives as in all other armed conflicts combined— from the Revolution to Vietnam.

Confederate earthwork fortification with field cannon, Atlanta, Georgia (National Archives Photo Collection).

This first modern major war was visually preserved by numerous photographers. Although pictures had been taken in earlier conflicts, the Civil War was the first massively documented clash of arms in which nearly a million images were captured. During wartime, the craft of taking photographs was a complex and very time-consuming matter. Usually, a team of two photographers arrived at the site. One of them prepared the chemicals and poured them on a glass plate. After the chemicals had time to evaporate, the glass plate was sensitized by being immersed in a bath solution in total darkness. The plate was then placed in a holder and inserted in the camera which had been put into position and focused by the other photographer. Because of the relatively long exposure time of several seconds, the "living objects"—often soldiers posing before or after battle—were not allowed to move; otherwise the objects would have appeared blurred or out of focus. The exposure of the plate and the development of the photograph had to be completed within a matter of minutes. These fragile glass plates had to be treated with utmost care after the development process. This

Wounded soldiers after battle at Fredericksburg, Virginia. Some of these men lost their legs or arms.

was—in times of war and under combat conditions—often a challenging task. As a result, it is miraculous that thousands of photographs have survived to this day. They are invaluable eyewitnesses to a war that helped shape modern America.

Covering the entire period of the Civil War, many of these images—known as "stereographs"—were either taken by so-called "stereo cameras" or cameras placed side-by-side on the same stand. Compelling images of death on the battlefields, the destruction of cities, railroads and bridges, visualize the devastating effects of this epic conflict. There are numerous individual and group portraits of soldiers, generals, civilians, and politicians; images of servicemen relaxing in camps or being cared for in hospitals, drilling in the field, and preparing for attack. Some photographs show African Americans who had fled slavery, as well as African Americans serving in the Union's armed forces.

The ironclad USS *Monitor*, after her famous battle with the CSS *Virginia* (ex-*Merrimac*), is depicted, as well as other warships of the time. The creation of "stereographs"—the 19th century equivalent of today's three-dimensional imaging—is almost as old as the craft of photography itself, because even early photographers wanted to preserve the 3D effect that only our eyes can capture. Stereoscopy—also known as stereoscopic or 3D imaging—is a technique for creating the illusion of depth in an image by presenting two offset images separately to the left and right eyes of the viewer. Both of these 2D offset images are then combined in the brain to give the perception of three-dimensional depth when viewed with a stereograph viewer. During the second half of the 19th century, and well into the 20th century, countless stereographs of nearly every photographic topic were taken, and used for presentations in science, education, art, and entertainment. Because of their journalistic style, stereographs provide an immediate and graphic look at the Civil War.

Now, more than 150 years after the outbreak of the Civil War, it is possible to digitally restore and convert surviving stereographs into 3D images which easily can be viewed with red-cyan-

colored glasses in order to experience an impressive three-dimensional effect. *The Civil War—The 3D Experience* takes the reader on a journey back in time when an epic four-year conflict shaped the history of the modern United States. By viewing the historical images in 3D, which are from the collection of the U.S. Library of Congress (unless otherwise noted), the reader will get the impression of being where the war took place—on the battlefield at Gettysburg, aboard the famous USS *Monitor*, at a soldiers' hospital, or in the ruins of once proud cities.

However, it is often the photographer's intention to communicate an idea or emotion with his photograph. Although camera lenses capture our world impartially, it is the photographer who deliberates and finally chooses a motif and how to depict it, thus focusing on creating

Entered according to Act of Congress, in the year 1862, by Gardner & Gibson, in the Clerk's Office of the District Court of the District of Columbia.

In this graphic photograph, the rifle was probably placed next to the body by the photographer.

a memorable image that can communicate a particularly intended message. As a result, there is evidence that Civil War photographers sometimes "rearranged" their photos, such as placing an artillery shell or rifle next to the mutilated body of a fallen soldier. Moreover, the words accompanying a photograph in captions may also influence the way we interpret an image.

This innovative book provides an insight into the numerous different facets of the American Civil War—in 3D. May this publication contribute to the commemoration of this conflict, and may we never forget the ultimate sacrifice made by so many.

I want to express my special gratitude to Dr. Robert K. Sutton, the National Park Service's chief historian, for writing the preface for this book.

Ingo Bauernfeind

Crew members of the ironclad USS *Monitor* posing in front of the rotating gun turret, which is covered with an awning.

HOW TO VIEW 3D ANAGLYPHS:

Now, please feel free to put on your 3D glasses, and view the image before you. It might take a few seconds to adjust your eyes to the photo, so it might help to focus on one object first, and then let your eyes "wander" through the photo.

NOTE

Only use the 3D glasses for viewing the anaglyphs in this book. Please be aware that the use of 3D glasses may cause momentary headache or a feeling of dizziness. As a result, please do not drive or operate machinery until feeling better. The author/publisher asks for your understanding that he cannot be held liable for any damages that may be caused to you or a third party through the use of 3D glasses.

NOVEMBER 1860
PRESIDENTIAL ELECTION

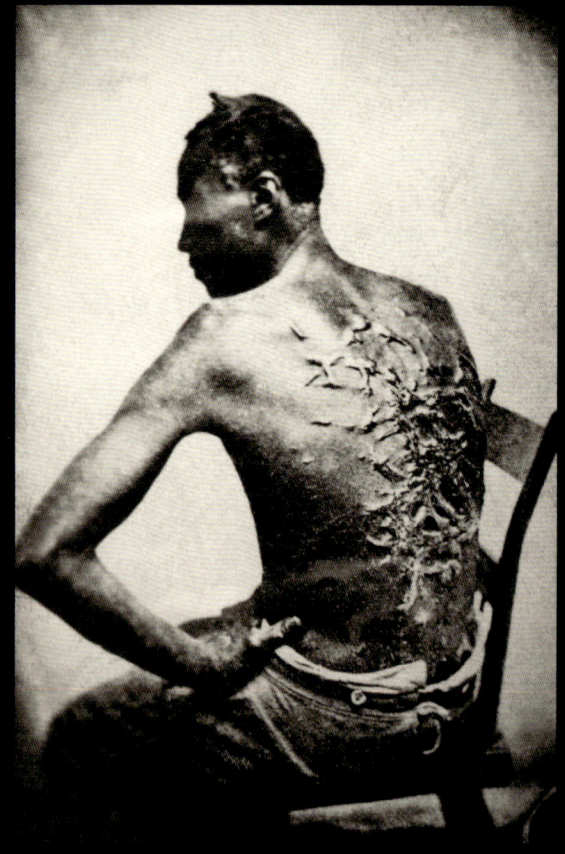

The American Civil War's causes were complex, and have been controversial since the conflict's outbreak. Since the 1850s, slavery was the central source of escalating political tension in the United States. While the Republican Party was determined to prevent the spread of slavery, numerous leaders in Southern states had threatened to secede from the Union if the Republican candidate, Abraham Lincoln, won the 1860 election: Lincoln was a known opponent of the spread of slavery into the territories. Following his victory in November, many Southern whites felt that secession was their only option. The first state to leave the Union was South Carolina in December 1860.

FEBRUARY 1861
SOUTHERN SECESSION

South Carolina's secession was followed by six additional states— Mississippi, Florida, Alabama, Georgia, Louisiana, and Texas. On February 4, these seven states formed the Confederate States of America with Jefferson Davis as president, and a constitution to govern its affairs.

Interior view of an empty slave pen in Alexandria, Virginia. It was once used by Price, Birch & Co., one of the country's largest slave trading companies. This photograph was taken after Union troops had occupied the city and converted the pen into a prison. Photograph by Brady & Co.

THE SOUTH TAKES CONTROL OF FEDERAL FORTS

When Lincoln's predecessor, outgoing President James Buchanan, whose term ended on March 4, refused to surrender federal forts located within the territory of the seceding states, Southern troops took control of them. The Union, however, continued to hold Fort Sumter, in Charleston, South Carolina Harbor, and Fort Pickens near Pensacola in Florida.

Fort Pickens, Pensacola Harbor, Florida.

ABRAHAM LINCOLN'S INAUGURATION

The bible used by Abraham Lincoln for his oath of office during his first inauguration in 1861.

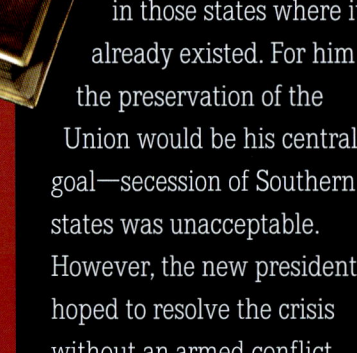

At his inauguration on March 4, Lincoln stated that he didn't want to interfere with the institution of slavery in those states where it already existed. For him the preservation of the Union would be his central goal—secession of Southern states was unacceptable. However, the new president hoped to resolve the crisis without an armed conflict.

RIGHT Inauguration of Abraham Lincoln as the 16th president of the United States of America at the U.S. Capitol, Washington, DC. Note the incomplete dome.

When the Republican candidate Abraham Lincoln won the 1860 election, be became the nation's 16th president.

This photograph was taken by Lewis E. Walker in February 1865—two months before Lincoln's assassination.

APRIL 1861
ATTACK ON FORT SUMTER, SOUTH CAROLINA

Forewarned by President Lincoln that he was sending a supply fleet to Fort Sumter, Confederate forces decided to take action before the arrival of the relief ships. The fort's Union commander, Major Robert Anderson, refused an ultimatum to abandon the

fort, so Confederates began firing on the morning of April 12. Following a 34-hour bombardment Major Anderson surrendered. The Civil War had begun.

TOP Confederate bombardment of Fort Sumter, April 12, 1861.

RIGHT Fort Sumter after its surrender. Note the Confederate flag.

APRIL 1861
FOUR ADDITIONAL SOUTHERN STATES JOIN THE CONFEDERACY

The Confederacy's attack on Fort Sumter prompted four more states—Virginia, Arkansas, Tennessee, and North Carolina—to join the seven seceded states. After Virginia's secession from the Union, Richmond became the capital. These eleven states now formed the Confederate States of America ("the Confederacy"), whereas the other 25 states continued to support the federal government in Washington, DC ("the Union").

$100 bank note of the Confederate States of America. Note the slaves depicted on top.

The north wall of Fort Sumter, near Charleston, South Carolina. The Civil War began when Confederate troops attacked this fortification on April 12, 1861. Note the breach caused by Confederate artillery fire. It was later patched with gabions. Photograph by George N. Barnard.

JUNE 1861
FOUR SLAVE STATES REMAIN IN THE UNION

Despite their retention of slavery, the states of Delaware, Maryland, Kentucky, and Missouri remained in the Union. A combination of political maneuvers and military pressure from the North kept these states from joining the Confederacy— although their loyalties were divided.

General Winfield Scott, the Union's commander-in-chief at the war's beginning.

JULY 1861
THE FIRST BATTLE OF BULL RUN (MANASSAS), VIRGINIA

Public demand urged Winfield Scott, the Union's commander-in-chief, to attack the South before he believed his "green" troops were adequately trained. He ordered General Irvin McDowell to advance on Confederate troops stationed at Manassas Junction, Virginia. McDowell attacked them on July 21. Although his federal troops were initially successful, the introduction of Confederate reinforcements led to their defeat and a chaotic retreat toward Washington, DC. When President Lincoln began to realize that this conflict could turn into a protracted war, he saw the need for more effectively organized and better trained troops.

Capture of Ricketts' Battery
by Sidney E. King (1906 – 2002)

A Union soldier standing at attention (probably posing for the photographer) in front of a little stone church in Centreville, Virginia. Union troops passed this place on their way to the battlefield at Bull Run near Manassas Junction in July 1861. After the engagement, the church was briefly used as a hospital for wounded soldiers. Photograph by George N. Barnard.

JULY 1861
BLOCKADING THE SOUTHERN COAST

As part of the overall Union strategy, its navy established a blockade to stop Confederate shipping commerce. At first, because of lack of naval vessels, it was mostly a "paper" blockade, but eventually, as the Union's military began to capture Confederate harbors, and as the Union added more ships with a better coordinated effort, the blockade became more and more effective.

AUGUST 1861
BATTLE OF WILSON'S CREEK (OAK HILLS), MISSOURI

The Battle of Wilson's Creek, also known as the Battle of Oak Hills, was the first major Civil War battle fought west of the Mississippi River. During the engagement, the first Union general, Nathaniel Lyon, was killed in combat. The bloody Southern victory on August 10, 1861, focused greater national attention on the Civil War in Missouri.

General Nathaniel Lyon of the Union who was killed on August 10, 1861 (National Park Service Photo Collection).

Captain Samuel F. Du Pont who later would become an admiral.

NOVEMBER 1861
THE BATTLE OF PORT ROYAL, SOUTH CAROLINA

On November 7, a large fleet of Union warships under the command of Captain Samuel F. Du Pont put the Confederate artillery of Fort Walker and Fort Beauregard out of action. This enabled General Thomas W. Sherman's Union troops (the U.S. Army) to take control of Port Royal and South Carolina's sea islands.

Union warships bombarding Port Royal.

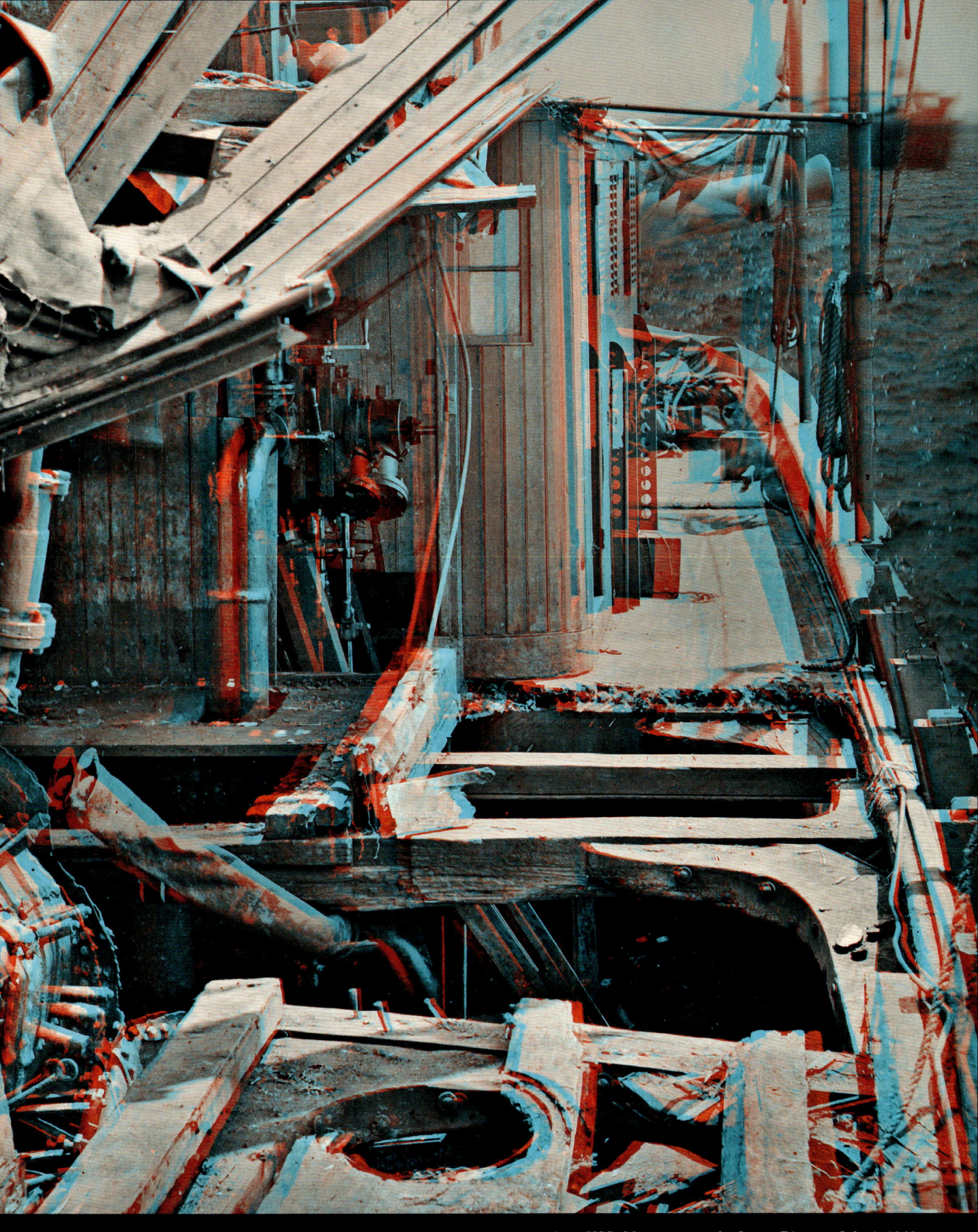

Deck of the Confederate gunboat CSS *Teaser*, which was captured by the Union gunboat USS *Maratanza* on the James River on July 4, 1862. Note the battle damage suffered during the engagement. The advent of armored ironclad ships during the Civil War would make wooden vessels such as the *Teaser* and the *Maratanza* eventually obsolete. Photograph by James F. Gibson.

CHANGING OF THE GUARD

After General Scott's retirement, General George B. McClellan became the Union's new supreme commander (general-in-chief).

Union officers in camp.

General George B. McClellan of the Union.

MARCH 1862
BATTLE OF PEA RIDGE (ELKHORN TAVERN), ARKANSAS

On March 7, Union forces led by General Samuel R. Curtis moved south from central Missouri and drove Confederate forces into northwestern Arkansas. However, the Confederates under the command of General Earl Van Dorn launched a counteroffensive, hoping to recapture northern Arkansas and Missouri. In a two-day battle, the Union held off the Confederate attack on the first day and drove Van Dorn's forces off the field on the following day. The battle's outcome cemented the Union's control of Missouri and northern Arkansas.

General Earl Van Dorn of the Confederacy.

General Samuel R. Curtis of the Union.

Confederate fort at Centreville, Virginia, nearby Bull Run (Manassas Junction) during the winter, 1861 – 1862. Significantly fortified by the Confederacy, Manassas Junction served as a supply depot for both sides at various points in the war. Note the "wooden guns": although resembling actual cannons, the so-called "Quaker Gun" was a simple wooden log, often painted black, used to deceive enemy troops. Misleading the adversary as to an emplacement's strength was an effective delaying tactic. The name derives from the religious group of Quakers. Photograph by George N. Barnard.

MARCH 1862
LINCOLN REMOVES MCCLELLAN FROM SUPREME COMMAND

By March, President Lincoln was growing more and more frustrated with General McClellan's inactivity. For his part, McClellan started devising a plan to transport his army to the Peninsula (southeastern Virginia) to drive on Richmond. But, Lincoln was concerned that at that time, the Confederate Army was still in Northern Virginia, and could potentially march on unprotected Washington, DC. McClellan was eventually replaced with General Henry W. Halleck.

TOP LEFT Confederate White House in Richmond, Virginia. Home of President Jefferson Davis.

TOP RIGHT The White House, Washington, DC.

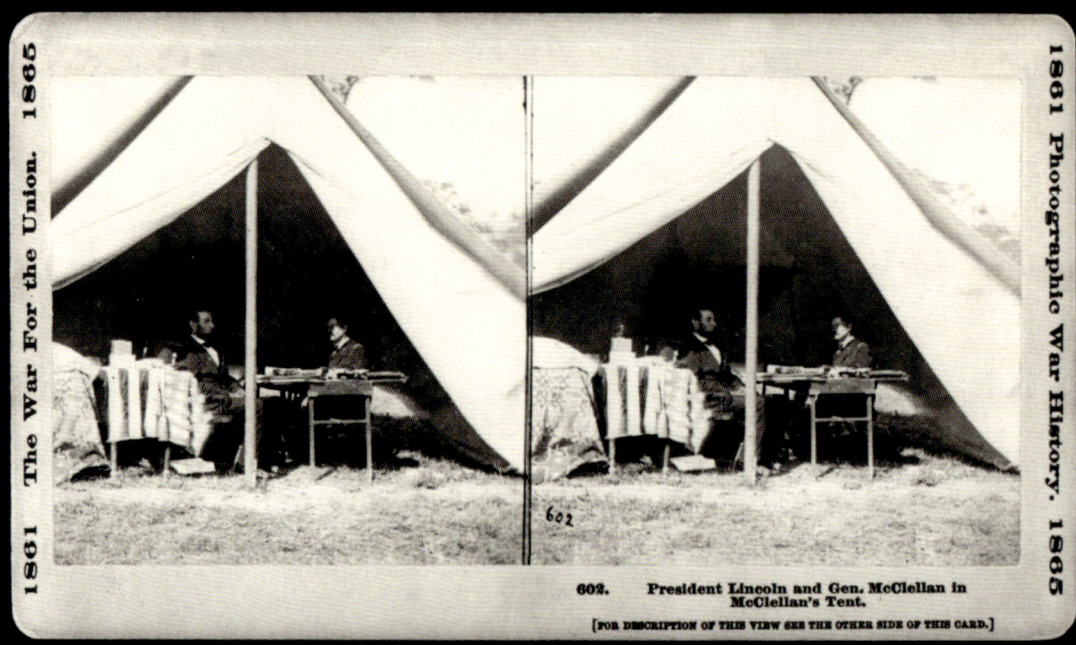

Original stereoscopic card showing President Lincoln and General McClellan. The three-dimensional anaglyph can be viewed on the opposite page.

Lincoln and McClellan during a meeting in the general's tent. This photo was actually taken two weeks after the Battle of Antietam, which took place in September 1862—four months after the president had removed McClellan from supreme command. Photograph by Alexander Gardner.

BATTLE OF THE USS *MONITOR* AND THE CSS *VIRGINIA* (EX-USS *MERRIMAC*)

In order to challenge the Union's supremacy at sea, Confederate naval engineers reconstructed the scuttled hull of the former Union's frigate USS *Merrimac* into an ironclad warship, and renamed it the CSS *Virginia*. On March 9, after sinking two wooden Union warships off Norfolk, Virginia, she was attacked by the armored USS *Monitor*. The subsequent first naval engagement in history between ironclad ships led to a draw without a victor. However, it clearly demonstrated the superiority of ironclad vessels over wooden warships.

Line drawings of the USS *Monitor*, side and top view. (Naval Historical Center Collection).

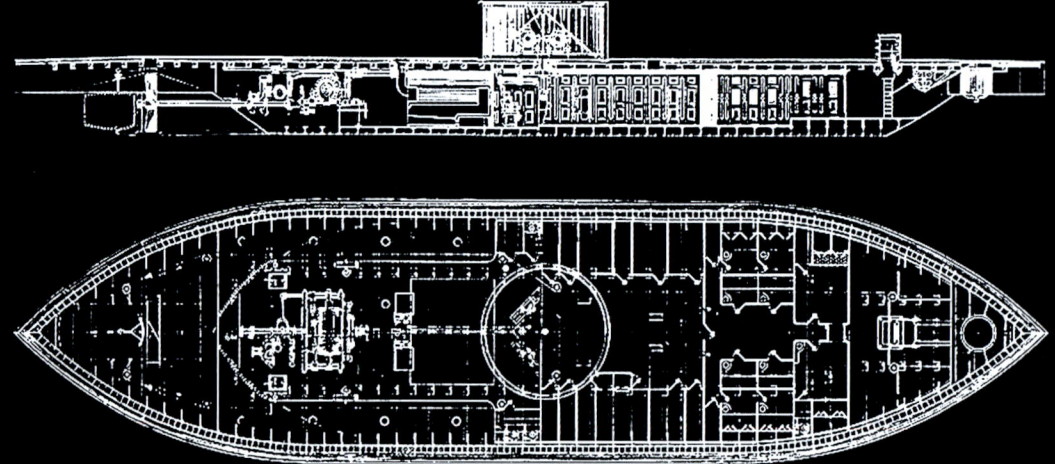

LEFT The CSS *Virginia* sinking the wooden Union frigate USS *Cumberland*.

RIGHT The famous battle between the CSS *Virginia* (left) and the USS *Monitor* (right) off Hampton Roads on March 9, 1862.

The USS *Monitor*'s gun turret after battle. Note the dents at left. The ship's design was well-suited for river combat, but its low freeboard and heavy turret made it highly unseaworthy in rough waters. As a result, she sank during a storm off Cape Hatteras, North Carolina, on December 31, 1862. In recent years, the ship's revolutionary revolving gun turret and other parts from the wreck site were recovered. They are now on display at the Mariners' Museum of Newport News, Virginia. Photograph by James F. Gibson.

APRIL 1862
THE BATTLE OF SHILOH, TENNESSEE

On April 6, the western Confederate Army launched a surprise attack on Union forces under General Ulysses S. Grant at Shiloh, Tennessee, inflicting heavy casualties and nearly bringing the Union troops to the brink of defeat by the end of the day. However, during the night, arriving Union reinforcements strengthened Grant's bloodied command, enabling a Union counterattack, which won the battle in a second day of brutal fighting.

Shiloh was, however, the most sobering battle to that point in the war. By the end of the battle, there were 23,746 total casualties on both sides combined (killed, wounded, and missing), which was far greater than the casualties in any Civil War battle to that point, and greater than all previous American conflicts combined.

General Ulysses S. Grant of the Union.

TOP The Battle of Shiloh, Tennessee.
RIGHT Present-day image of Union field artillery at Shiloh National Military Park, Tennessee (Photograph by Carol M. Highsmith / Library of Congress).

Union soldiers with 13-inch-mortars. Early means of mass production and significant advances in the design of weapons enabled Civil War armies to unleash a ferocity on the battlefields never seen before, thus killing thousands within minutes. Due to its stronger industrial capacity, the Union had a significant advantage over the Confederacy in the mass production of arms. Photograph by James F. Gibson.

APRIL 1862
ATTACK ON FORT PULASKI, GEORGIA

On April 10-11, Union troops besieged and battered Fort Pulaski, a masonry fortification located near the mouth of the Savannah River (Georgia). General Quincy A. Gillmore devised a plan to capture Fort Pulaski with a new weapon, the rifled cannon. Within 30 hours, the walls of the fort were breached, and Confederate Colonel Charles H. Olmstead surrendered. With this defeat, the masonry fortification was soon considered obsolete.

Fort Pulaski's battered exterior walls.

General Quincy A. Gillmore of the Union.

Aerial photograph of Fort Pulaski today. Note the damaged walls (National Park Service Photo Collection).

Interior view of Fort Pulaski's breached wall after it was taken by Union forces. Despite its massive construction, it couldn't withstand the effective shelling by field artillery. A Union soldier is visible behind a partly buried casemate gun, which couldn't prevent the bastion's fall. Photograph by Timothy H. O'Sullivan.

APRIL 1862
THE BEGINNING OF THE PENINSULAR CAMPAIGN (VIRGINIA)

In April, Union General McClellan—now in command of the Army of the Potomac—ordered his troops to depart Northern Virginia and launch the Peninsular Campaign. By May 4, he occupied Yorktown, Virginia. At Williamsburg, Confederate forces prevented McClellan from meeting the core of the Confederate Army. McClellan halted his troops, and awaited reinforcements. He was under the illusion that his forces were outnumbered, when, in fact, his army outnumbered the Confederates by nearly 2 to

Street view of Yorktown after being occupied by Union troops.

APRIL 1862
SEIZING OF NEW ORLEANS, LOUISIANA

Union Navy Flag Officer David G. Farragut commanded an assault up the Mississippi River and by April 25, his forces were in control of New Orleans, Louisiana.

Flag Officer David G. Farragut of the Union Navy (National Archives Photo Collection).

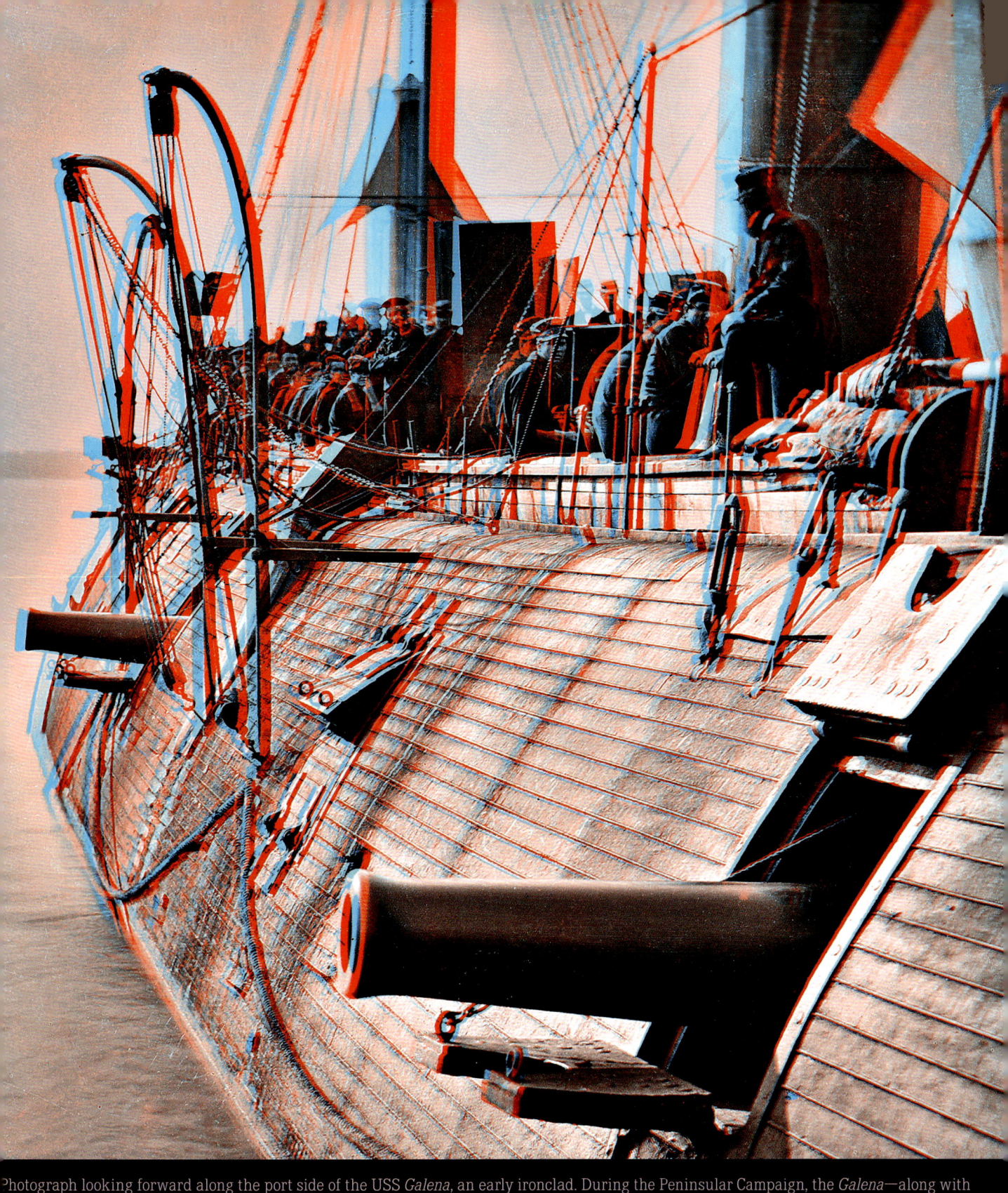

Photograph looking forward along the port side of the USS *Galena*, an early ironclad. During the Peninsular Campaign, the *Galena*—along with the USS *Monitor* and three more ships—steamed up the James River to test the defenses of the fort on Drewry's Bluff near Richmond, Virginia, on May 15, 1862. The fort's strong defenses blunted the Union's advance, and Richmond remained safe. This image of the *Galena* was taken shortly after her action showing the muzzles of her guns, horizontally-laid interlocking iron side armor, as well as members of her crew. Note the plugged

MARCH – MAY 1862
GENERAL JACKSON DEFEATS UNION TROOPS

General Thomas J. "Stonewall" Jackson, the Confederate commander of forces stationed in the Shenandoah Valley, harassed Union troops up and down the valley, eventually forcing them to retreat across the Potomac River. As a result, Union troops had to be mobilized to protect Washington, DC.

General Thomas J. "Stonewall" Jackson of the Confederacy.

Heavy artillery emplacement at Washington, DC.

Washington, DC. The aqueduct bridge and Georgetown viewed from the Virginia bank.

Washington, DC, viewed from Mason's Island. Note the ferryboat carrying wagons with the aqueduct bridge in the background. During the Civil War, Confederate troops were able to attack the capital at Fort Stevens in July 1864. Photo by George N. Barnard.

JUNE 1862
THE BATTLE OF SEVEN PINES (FAIR OAKS), VIRGINIA

On May 31, Confederate troops attacked Union forces at Seven Pines (Fair Oaks). Reinforcements arriving at the last minute saved the Union from a serious defeat. During the battle, the Confederate commander General Joseph E. Johnston was wounded, so the command of the Army of Northern Virginia was transferred to General Robert E. Lee.

LEFT General Joseph E. Johnston of the Confederate Army (National Archives).

GHT General Robert E. Lee, Johnston's successor.

Drawing of the evacuation of wounded Union soldiers during the Battle of Seven Pines.

A group photo of four Union Army officers posing for the camera in front of a field cannon. Note that in this carefully arranged photograph each man is leaning against the cannon in an attempt to avoid, or at least reduce, any body movements that could blur the image due to the long exposure time of 19th century cameras. This photo doesn't show the cruelty and hardship of war, it appears rather solemn. However, the following three-dimensional image on page 41 will present a completely different image of war. Interestingly, both photos were taken by the same photographer, James F. Gibson.

JUNE – JULY 1862
THE SEVEN DAYS' BATTLES

Between June 26 and July 2, Union and Confederate troops engaged each other in a series of battles: Mechanicsville (June 26), Gaines' Mill (June 27), Savage's Station (June 29), Frayser's Farm (Glendale, June 30), and Malvern Hill (July 1). General McClellan and his Army of the Potomac had reached the outskirts of Richmond, but following the Seven Days' Battles, he began to retreat, eventually pulling his troops out of the Peninsula. The campaign was over.

Unburied dead soldiers on the battlefield of Gaines' Mill, which took place on June 27, 1862.

Private Edwin Francis Jemison served in the Confederate States Army. He was killed during the Battle of Malvern Hill at the age of seventeen.

THE BATTLE OF MALVERN HILL, VA. JULY 1ST 1862.
Charge of the 26th. New York Volunteers, at the Battle of Malvern Hill, July 1st 1862, and Capture of the Colors of the 14th Reg't N.C. Infantry.

of Malvern Hill, on July 1, 1862.

In contrast to the staged three-dimensional group photo on page 39, this image—taken shortly after the Battle of Gaines' Mill (June 27, 1862)—shows the misery of war without any extenuation. This rough-and-ready Union field hospital at Savage's Station is full of details showing soldiers with various wounds, getting treatment, or waiting to receive medical assistance.

Photo by James F. Gibson.

JULY 1862
A NEW COMMANDER FOR THE UNION ARMY

On July 11, General Henry W. Halleck became the general-in-chief of the Union Army. President Lincoln had removed General McClellan from that post in March 1862, leaving him in command of only the Army of the Potomac.

General Henry W. Halleck of the Union
(National Archives Photo Collection).

AUGUST 1862
GENERAL POPE'S CAMPAIGN

General John Pope
of the Union.

Frustrated with General McClellan, and concerned with the protection of Washington, DC, President Lincoln established a new army—the Army of Virginia—and brought in General John Pope as its commander. On August 28 – 30, Pope engaged the Confederates under General Lee in the Second Battle of Bull Run (Manassas). This was a stunning victory for the Confederates, and gave General Lee the impetus to invade the North. This led to the Battle of Antietam a little over two weeks later.

Drawing of the Second Battle of Bull Run (Manassas).

A soldier caught sleeping. The original caption says that this is Lieutenant Colonel Samuel W. Owen of the 3rd Pennsylvania Cavalry (Union Army). Photograph by Alexander Gardner.

SEPTEMBER 1862
FALL OF HARPERS FERRY, WEST VIRGINIA

General McClellan's Union troops defeated Confederate General Lee in the battles at South Mountain and Crampton's Gap in September. However, McClellan did not move quickly enough to save Harpers Ferry from a Confederate attack. The town, along with a great number of men and supplies, was taken by General Jackson on September 15. Because of Harpers Ferry's strategic location on the railroad and the nearby Shenandoah Valley, it was of vital interest for both the Union and the Confederacy. As a result, the Civil War was disastrous for the town, which changed hands several times until 1865.

Partly colorized photograph of an unidentified soldier in Union uniform with rifle.

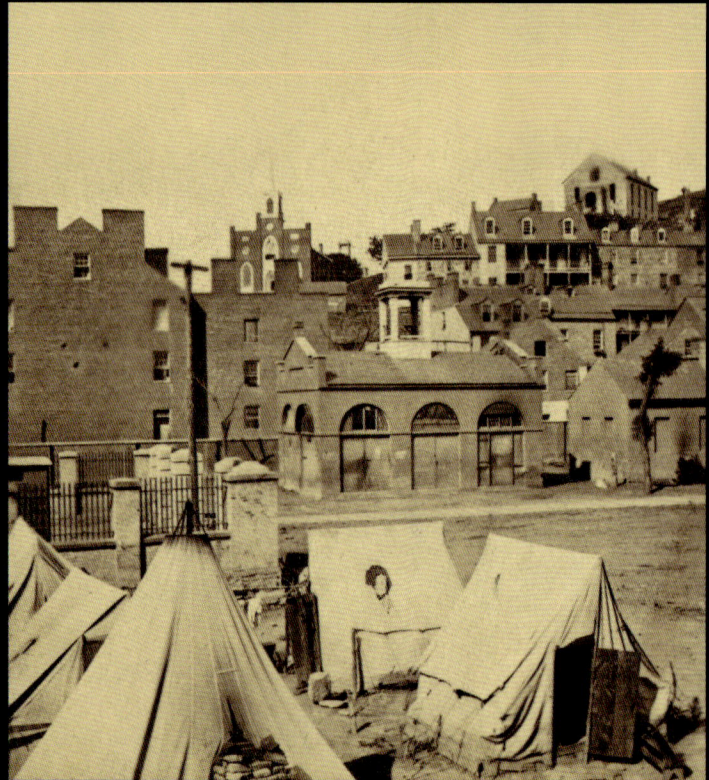

Harpers Ferry (formerly *Harper's Ferry*), ca. 1860. When Virginia joined the Confederacy in April 1861, the town's Union garrison destroyed the armory in order to prevent the Confederates from using it. However, locals saved the equipment, which the Confederate Army transferred to its capital, Richmond.

Rifles—such as the ones produced at Harpers Ferry—were the most common weapons used by both sides during the Civil War. Most of these weapons during that time were muzzle loaded rifled muskets that were loaded with small lead musket balls (Minié balls) and black powder.

THE BATTLE OF ANTIETAM (SHARPSBURG), MARYLAND

On September 17, General McClellan's Union troops attacked General Lee's Confederate forces near Sharpsburg, Maryland. This battle turned into the bloodiest day of the Civil War and in American history. There were more than 23,000 casualties. Technically, the battle ended in a draw, but since General Lee retreated to Virginia, it was considered a Union victory. This engagement convinced Great Britain and France, who were debating to officially recognize the secession states as the independent Confederate States of America, to reserve action, and gave President Lincoln the chance to announce his *Preliminary Emancipation Proclamation* (September 22), which would free all slaves in the Confederate states.

TOP Battle of Antietam on September 17, 1862.

RIGHT Casualties of the battle lined up for burial.

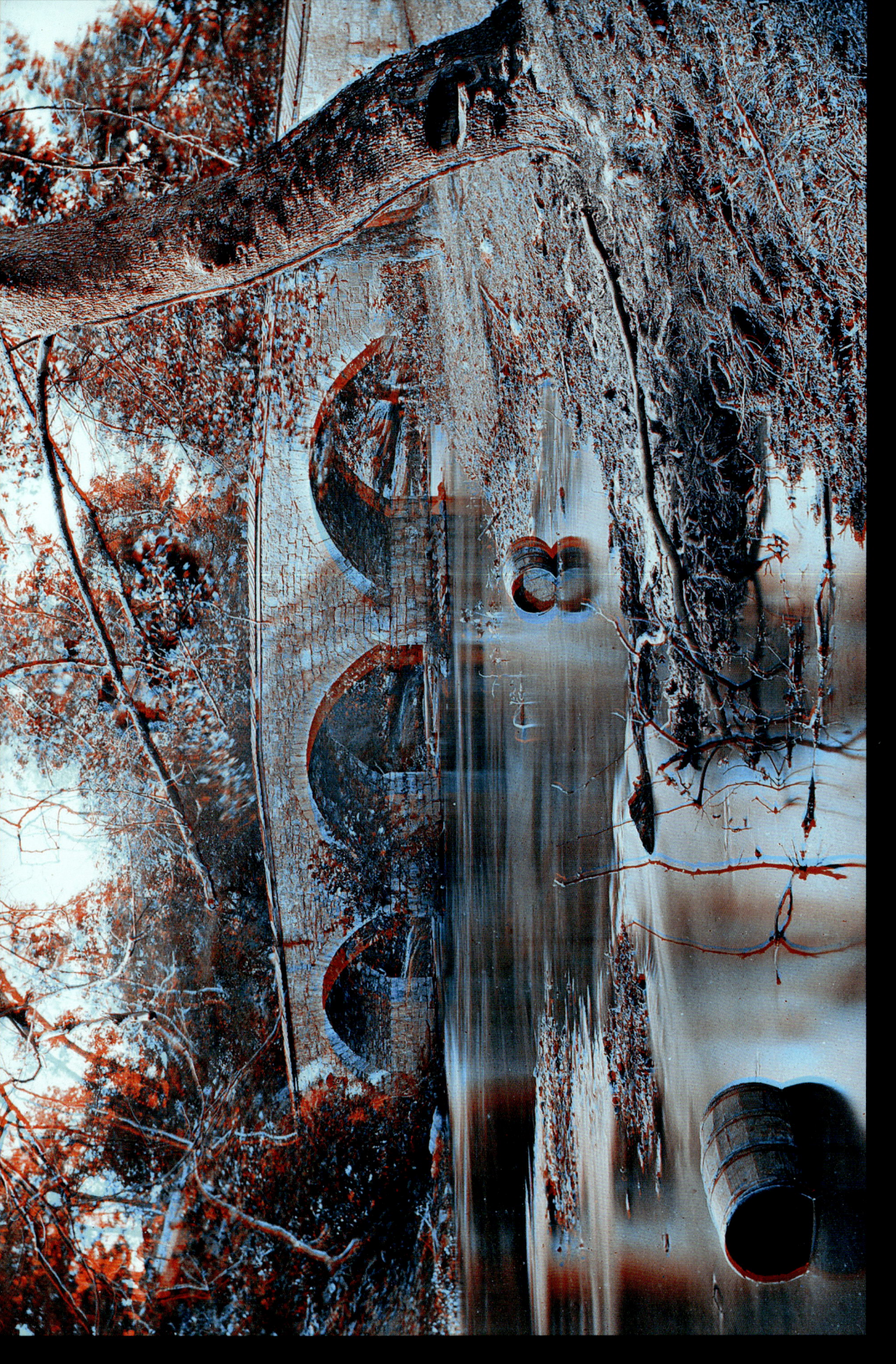

Crossing over Antietam Creek, this bridge played a key role in Battle of Antietam, when a small number of Confederate soldiers from Georgia for several hours were able to held off repeated attempts of Union troops to take the bridge by force. The bridge now bears the name of Union General Ambrose Burnside – Burnside's Bridge.

A dead Confederate soldier unburied, next to a Union soldier buried (right). Both are resting side by side—where they fell. The Union troops, which gained the control of the battlefield after General Lee's retreat, buried their own killed men first. Photograph by Alexander Gardner.

A primitive rough-and-ready field hospital for Confederate soldiers nearby Keedysville, Maryland. After the Battle of Antietam, many of these hospitals were hastily erected in order to take care of some of the thousands of wounded soldiers. Photograph by Alexander Gardner.

General John C. Caldwell of the Union (center) with his staff posing in camp near Antietam.
Note the U.S. flag covering the entrance of the tent. Photograph by Alexander Gardner.

DECEMBER 1862
THE BATTLE OF FREDERICKSBURG, VIRGINIA

Even with constant prodding, General McClellan was slow to follow President Lincoln's orders to pursue Confederate General Robert E. Lee across the Potomac River. Finally, in exasperation, Lincoln removed McClellan from command and replaced him with General Ambrose E. Burnside who had achieved success in other campaigns. Unlike McClellan, Burnside was aggressive, but his aggressiveness led to a stunning defeat in Fredericksburg, Virginia (December 11–15, 1862). Frustrated, Lincoln replaced Burnside with General Joseph Hooker.

Drawing of the Battle of Fredericksburg.

LEFT General Ambrose E. Burnside of the Union.
RIGHT General Joseph Hooker who became Burnside's successor.

Union General Burnside reading a newspaper at his corps headquarters in June 1864. The civilian sitting opposite Burnside is Mathew B. Brady, perhaps the best known Civil War photographer, who appears in other Civil War photographs as well. This photograph was taken by an unidentified employee of Brady.

President Abraham Lincoln at the first reading of the Emancipation Proclamation on July 22, 1862, painted by Francis B. Carpenter at the White House in 1864.

In order to calm the slave-holding border states fighting on the Union's side, Lincoln had to show caution concerning the institution in those states. But he, many of his supporters, numerous Union generals, as well as the enslaved people themselves, were moving toward the end of slavery as a war

aim. Beginning shortly after the war started, escaping slaves were welcomed into Union camps as "contraband of war." The growing movement toward emancipation was aided by the passage of the confiscation acts of 1861 and 1862. Lincoln was aware of the general public's increasing support of the eventual complete abolition, and therefore issued the *Emancipation Proclamation* on January 1, 1863. It declared that all slaves in areas still in rebellion were free.

President Lincoln's *Emancipation Proclamation*.

African American army cook at work. Men like him had fled slavery and were called "contrabands". Many would serve in the Union Army as servants or eventually as armed soldiers ("Colored troops").

MARCH 1863
THE FIRST CONSCRIPTION ACT

In order to overcome recruiting difficulties, an act was passed making all male adults between the ages of 20 and 45 liable for conscription into military service. By paying a fee or finding a substitute, service with the troops could be avoided, but this option was considered unfair to the poor. As a result, riots broke out in working-class districts of New York City. In the Confederate States, similar acts to draft men into military service drew challenges before five state supreme courts, although all five upheld them.

The draft riots in New York City. People sacking a clothing store (from: *Harper's Weekly,* August 1, 1863).

MAY 1863
THE BATTLE OF CHANCELLORSVILLE, VIRGINIA

On April 27, General Joseph Hooker crossed the Rappahannock River with his Union troops to attack General Lee's Confederate forces. Lee reacted by splitting his army in the face of superior numbers, and engaged the Union in a surprise attack on Hooker's far right flank. This operation and furious Confederate attacks the next day led to Hooker retreating over the river, and another stunning Confederate victory. But Confederate General Stonewall Jackson afterwards died of wounds he had received towards the end of directing the surprise attack. His loss was a heavy blow to the Confederacy.

General "Stonewall" Jackson being shot at the Battle of Chancellorsville on May 2, 1863.

For raiders and saboteurs, wooden river bridges were attractive targets, because they could be burned easily. Bridges often played a vital role in the maneuvering of troops and supplies from one side of a river to the other. To protect these vulnerable spans, they often were fortified with walls, watchtowers, and guns. Photograph by George N. Barnard.

MAY 1863
THE VICKSBURG CAMPAIGN, MISSISSIPPI

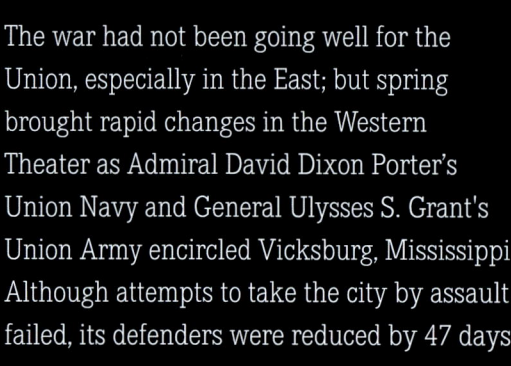

The war had not been going well for the Union, especially in the East; but spring brought rapid changes in the Western Theater as Admiral David Dixon Porter's Union Navy and General Ulysses S. Grant's Union Army encircled Vicksburg, Mississippi. Although attempts to take the city by assault failed, its defenders were reduced by 47 days of relentless siege, and Confederate General John C. Pemberton surrendered Vicksburg, along with its 30,000-man garrison, to General Grant on July 4, 1863. Port Hudson, Louisiana, quickly followed, putting the entire length of the Mississippi River under Union control and geographically splitting the Confederacy in two.

TOP General John C. Pemberton of the Confederacy.

RIGHT The Union's siege of Vicksburg, May 1863.

JUNE 1863
THE BIRTH OF THE STATE OF WEST VIRGINIA

When Virginia seceded, its western counties refused to join. As a result, this region of Virginia was eventually accepted into the Union as the state of West Virginia on June 20. It was the only state in the Union to secede from a Confederate state (Virginia) during the Civil War.

The State Seal of West Virginia by Joseph H. Diss Debar.

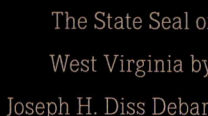

After the entire Mississippi River had fallen into Union hands, federal ships were able to move troops and supplies widely unhindered to various battle sites and strategic locations.

JUNE – JULY 1863
THE GETTYSBURG CAMPAIGN, PENNSYLVANIA

After his victory at Chancellorsville, General Lee decided to again take the war into Union territory. President Lincoln replaced Hooker with General George G. Meade, who immediately started pursuing Lee after he had crossed the Potomac. As happened with many Civil War battles, neither the Union nor the Confederate forces planned to collide at the town of Gettysburg, but they did, which became one of the largest and most deadly battles of the war. After three days of intensive fighting, starting on July 1, the Union won a decisive victory. Many historians call this battle the High Water Mark of the Confederacy, for although the war would continue for nearly two more years, the Confederacy had reached its pinnacle of power, which it would not really regain for the remainder of the war. Also, the staggering losses at Gettysburg—over 50,000 casualties including nearly 8,000 deaths—further depleted both armies, but the Confederacy could ill-afford to continue losing men at this level.

Painting showing "Pickett's Charge", the famous Confederate infantry assault against Union positions at Cemetery Ridge on July 3, 1863—the last day of the Battle of Gettysburg. The futile charge was named after George Pickett, one of three Confederate generals leading the assault.

BOTTOM RIGHT General George G. Meade of the Union.

BOTTOM LEFT Three Confederate prisoners of war, photographed after the Gettysburg Campaign.

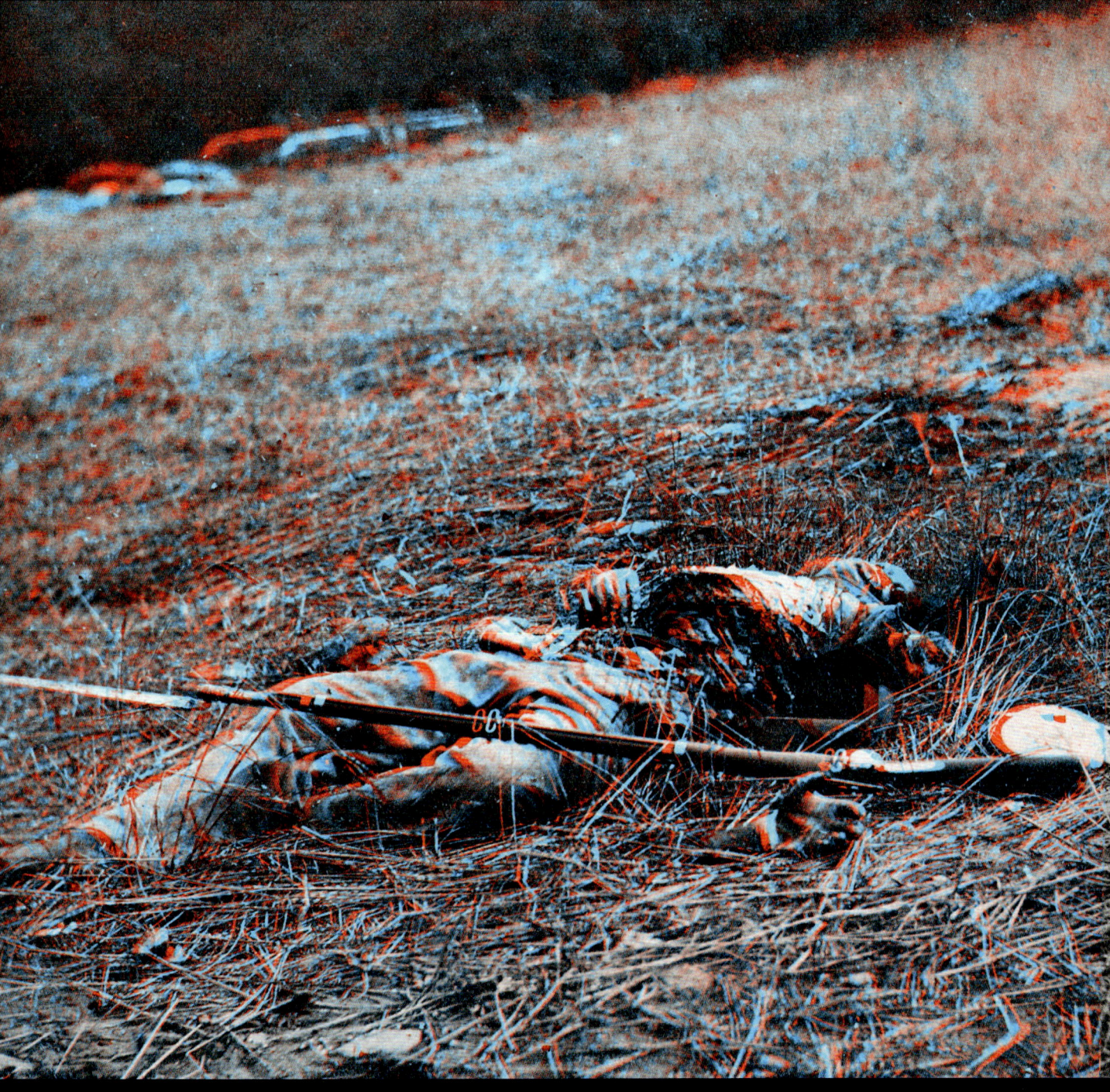

One of the most graphic images of the Civil War, if not of any recorded conflict in history. The position of the projectile (left) and the rifle suggest that this could be a manipulated photograph indicating that this Confederate soldier was killed by artillery fire. There is evidence that some Civil War photographers "rearranged" their images in an attempt of dramatizing the visual effect. However, this body could also have been disfigured by wild animals looking for food on the site following the battle. Photograph by Alexander Gardner.

Bodies of Confederate soldiers who died during the Gettysburg Campaign. Note the photographer's wagon at left.

SEPTEMBER 1863
THE BATTLE OF CHICKAMAUGA, GEORGIA

The Battle of Chickamauga (September 18–20, 1863).

On September 18, Union and Confederate troops engaged each other near Chickamauga Creek near the Tennessee-Georgia border. Union General George H. Thomas earned the nickname of the "Rock of Chickamauga" for holding back Confederate forces that had broken through a large gap in the Union line. With his defensive stand, the Union Army was able to retreat to Chattanooga, and avert what could have been a complete Confederate victory.

NOVEMBER 1863
THE BATTLE OF CHATTANOOGA, TENNESSEE

On November 23–25, Union forces under General Grant's command were able to push General Braxton Bragg's Confederate troops away from Chattanooga and its vital railroad center. This victory enabled General Sherman to launch the Atlanta Campaign.

LEFT General George H. Thomas of the Union.

CENTER General Braxton Bragg of the Confederacy.

RIGHT General James Longstreet of the Confederacy (National Archives).

NOVEMBER – DECEMBER 1863
THE SIEGE OF KNOXVILLE, TENNESSEE

The difficult strategic situation of the Union's armies after retreating from Chickamauga enabled Confederate General Bragg to detach troops under the command of General James Longstreet, which forced Union General Ambrose Burnside to withdraw from Eastern Tennessee. Burnside's troops marched to Knoxville, and defended it successfully against Confederate attacks.

Field artillery provided an enormous firepower. It could be moved by horses or even by men. Once in position, its shelling could wreak havoc at enemy emplacements and kill hundreds, if not thousands of soldiers. However, due to their weight, in bad weather those cannons could get stuck on dirt roads, thus slowing down an advance or retreat. These cannons are probably light 12-pounder "Napoleon", the war's most popular smoothbore cannon used by both the Union and Confederate armies. The cannon acquired its nickname after being modeled on a lightweight, maneuverable field gun that was developed in France under Napoleon III. After the war, many of these guns ended up as artifacts in Civil War museums or in historic battlefield parks. Photograph by James F. Gibson.

MAY 1864
GRANT'S WILDERNESS BATTLE

After being given command of all Union armies, General Grant opted to travel with the Army of the Potomac, essentially sharing its command with General George Meade. The mission was to fight Lee's Confederate forces in Virginia until their destruction.

The Battle of the Wilderness (May 5–7, 1864).

U.S. 5-cent stamp commemorating the Battle of the Wilderness (U.S. Post Office, 1964).

Grant's first encounter with Lee was an inconclusive two-day battle in the Wilderness. The South suffered less casualties than the North, but unlike Grant's troops, it could not replace them, and Grant kept moving southward rather than retreating.

MAY 1864
THE BATTLE OF SPOTSYLVANIA, VIRGINIA

Grant's and Meade's army continued to attack Lee's Confederate troops. At Spotsylvania Court House, Virginia, a two-week battle ensued, leading to new horrors in sustained bloodletting, and an inconclusive tactical outcome, but closing with another southward move by the undaunted Union Army.

Dead Confederate soldier near Spotsylvania Court House, Virginia.

General Grant meets with his staff and General Meade's at Massaponax Church, Spotsylvania County, Virginia, on May 21, 1864.

Grant (second from left) can be seen leaning over Meade's shoulder, studying a map. Note the supply wagons in the background.

Photograph by Timothy H. O'Sullivan.

THE BATTLE OF COLD HARBOR, VIRGINIA

The Battle of Cold Harbor (May 31–June 12, 1864) ended direct maneuvering by the Union Army against the Confederate capital at Richmond. After 18,000 casualties and prolonged misery in the trenches, the armies left Cold Harbor and moved south across the James River. Cold Harbor concluded the fearsome Overland Campaign and inaugurated the final phase of the war in central Virginia—a bitter contest around Petersburg.

Drawing depicting Union soldiers loading a mortar during the Battle of Cold Harbor.

Battle of Cold Harbor (May 31 - June 12, 1864).

After battle, the dead often were hastily buried in temporary shallow graves. When the Civil War finally ended, many remains were exhumed in order to give them proper burials. Photograph by John Reekie.

THE SIEGE OF PETERSBURG, VIRGINIA

Grant hoped to take Petersburg, Virginia. From there he planned to attack nearby Richmond, the Confederacy's capital. When the assault failed, a ten-month siege ensued, killing thousands on both sides.

Interior view of Confederate defense works.

The town of Petersburg, Virginia.

General Jubal A. Early of the Confederacy.

JULY 1864

CONFEDERATE TROOPS APPROACH WASHINGTON, DC

Confederate troops under the command of General Jubal A. Early marched into Maryland in order to relieve the pressure on Lee's embattled forces. Early managed to get as close as five miles from Washington, DC, but Union troops drove him back to Virginia on July 13.

Union 13-inch Seacoast mortar nicknamed "The Dictator" photographed with its crew in September 1864 during the Siege of Petersburg. Mortars like the one pictured above were indirect fire weapons capable of firing explosive projectiles in high arcing trajectories. "The Dictator" could throw its 200-pound shell almost 2 1/2 miles.

AUGUST 1864
GENERAL SHERMAN'S ATLANTA CAMPAIGN

When Union General William T. Sherman's troops departed Chattanooga, Tennessee, they soon were attacked by Confederate General Joseph Johnston's forces. Although Sherman's troops were almost twice the size of the Confederates' forces, Johnston was able to hold off the Union. However, his tactics prompted the supreme command to replace Johnston with General John B. Hood. When Hood was defeated, he surrendered Atlanta, Georgia, on September 1, and Sherman occupied the city the following day. This success was a boost for the Union's morale.

NOVEMBER 1864
SHERMAN'S MARCH TO THE SEA

Sherman's troops continued to march through Georgia in an attempt to reach the sea, but this meant that his soldiers cut themselves off from their source of supplies. As a result, they had to feed themselves off the land they would occupy during their advance. When they passed through Georgia, they destroyed public buildings, railroads, bridges, factories, and other structures.

LEFT Sherman's men destroying railroad tracks in Atlanta.

RIGHT A shell-damaged house in Atlanta.

Federal soldiers gathered around a field gun inside a Confederate fort captured by the Union nearby Atlanta. This photo gives an idea about the construction of field fortifications during the Civil War. The individual gun emplacements were connected with narrow passageways. Note the wooden planks underneath the cannon—they were supposed to prevent the wheels from sinking into the mud and ensure a proper recoil movement after firing. The sandbags helped to hold off enemy projectiles. The x-shaped obstacles or palisades in the background made it harder for attacking troops to find their way into the fort. Photograph by George N. Barnard.

NOVEMBER 1864
REELECTION OF ABRAHAM LINCOLN

During the 1864 election, the Democratic Party nominated General George B. McClellan as its presidential candidate against Abraham Lincoln. The widespread war weariness, as well as continued criticism from the Peace Democrats who wanted to end the war, created doubt for Lincoln's victory. However, the occupation of Atlanta helped to boost the president's popularity, and he clearly defeated McClellan.

LEFT Campaign poster for Abraham Lincoln (left) and his running mate Andrew Johnson (vice-president).

RIGHT Campaign poster for George B. McClellan (left) and George H. Pendleton.

JANUARY 1865
THE UNION'S BOMBARDMENT OF FORT FISHER, NORTH CAROLINA

After a squadron of Union warships under the command of Admiral David D. Porter had bombarded Fort Fisher, North Carolina, General Alfred H. Terry's Union troops were able to take it on January 15. As a result, nearby Wilmington was sealed off as the last place of refuge for Confederate blockade runners.

LEFT Admiral David D. Porter of the Union Navy.

RIGHT General Alfred H. Terry of the Union.

JANUARY 1865
THE DEMISE OF THE CONFEDERACY

The efficient blockade of Confederate seaports as well as transportation difficulties led to dramatic shortages of food and supplies in the South. When starving soldiers began to desert the Confederacy's forces, President Jefferson Davis agreed to augment the shrinking troops with armed slaves, but this idea was never turned into action.

Confederate gun emplacement near the James River (Virginia). Artillery installations were erected in order to prevent strategically significant locations such as harbor entrances, river mouths, or cities from capture by the enemy.

FEBRUARY 1865
SHERMAN'S UNION TROOPS MARCH THROUGH NORTH AND SOUTH CAROLINA

When Union forces led by General Sherman marched from Georgia through North and South Carolina, they destroyed almost everything in their way.

Ruins of Charleston in 1865.

General Sherman on horseback.

FEBRUARY 1865
A LOST CHANCE FOR RECONCILIATION

LEFT Lithograph of President Abraham Lincoln, USA.

RIGHT Lithograph of President Jefferson Davis, CSA.

When Confederate President Jefferson Davis agreed to send delegates to a peace conference with President Lincoln, he insisted on the formal recognition of the Confederacy's independence as a prerequisite. When Lincoln refused to accept this, the conference was called off.

The shell-damaged town of Charleston, South Carolina, photographed during the last months of the war. Although the town had been bombarded and attacked, it did not fall to Union forces until the last months of the war. The Mills House at left seems to have remained widely intact. Photograph by George N. Barnard.

THE UNION'S BREAKTHROUGH AT PETERSBURG AND THE FALL OF RICHMOND, VIRGINIA

On March 29-30, the Union Army finally broke through the Confederate lines at Petersburg. General Lee sent word to Confederate President Jefferson Davis to evacuate Richmond. This was the beginning of the end. Federal troops reached Richmond on April 3, and took control of the city.

TOP Victorious Union soldiers posing in the breastworks of the Confederate Fort Mahone, Petersburg.

LEFT Richmond's Custom House (left) and the Capitol (center) after the end of the war.

Group or family of freed slaves ("Freedmen") in Richmond, Virginia, April 1865. The arrival of Union troops brought an end to slavery in the Confederate states. Photograph by Alexander Gardner.

GENERAL LEE'S SURRENDER AT APPOMATTOX COURT HOUSE, VIRGINIA

When General Lee's Confederate troops were soon surrounded, Union General Grant appealed to him to surrender. Eventually, on April 9, the two commanders met at the village of Appomattox Court House, Virginia, where Lee agreed on the terms of surrender.

The McLean House became the site where General Lee surrendered. Appomattox Court House, Virginia.

The Room in the McLean House, at Appomattox C.H., in which GEN.LEE surrendered to GEN.GRANT.

eneral Lee's surrender to General Grant on April 9, 1865.

Richmond, Virginia, the short-lived capital of the Confederate States of America, lays in ruins by the war's end. Visible is the destroyed railroad depot, once an important hub for the transportation of troops and supplies. Note the locomotive in the center.

THE ASSASSINATION OF PRESIDENT LINCOLN, WASHINGTON, DC

On April 14, while watching a performance of the play "Our American Cousin" at Ford's Theatre in Washington, DC, President Abraham Lincoln was shot by John W. Booth. The murderer, an actor from Maryland, was obsessed to avenge the Confederate defeat. Lincoln died from his wounds the next morning. After Booth had escaped to Virginia, he was found 11 days later, and fatally shot by a Union soldier, while being cornered in a burning barn. Eventually four individuals who were involved in the conspiracy to assassinate President Lincoln were hanged in Washington, DC.

Derringer pocket pistol used by Booth to assassinate Abraham Lincoln (National Park Service Museum Collection).

John Wilkes Booth, the assassin.

Lithograph of the assassination of Abraham Lincoln.

Execution of the four people condemned as conspirators (Mary Surratt, Lewis Powell, David Herold, and George Atzerodt) on July 7, 1865, at Fort McNair, Washington, DC.

The chair in the presidential box at Ford's Theatre, in which President Abraham Lincoln was assassinated on April 14, 1865. After being shot, the fatally wounded president was carried across the street to the Petersen House, where he died the next morning at the age of 56.

FINAL SURRENDERS OF REMAINING CONFEDERATE FORCES

Between the end of April and the end of May, remaining Confederate troops which hadn't joined General Lee's official surrender on April 9, were eventually defeated by Union forces. On May 10, Jefferson Davis was captured in Georgia. After four years of severe fighting, mostly within the Southern states, the Union was restored, and slavery was abolished everywhere in the nation. Although Davis was charged with treason, he was not tried, but stripped of his citizenship. Congress posthumously restored his citzenship in 1978—eighty-nine years after his death.

After President Lincoln's death, Andrew Johnson became his successor. On May 9, 1865, he officially declared a virtual end to the conflict.

Profile portrait of Jefferson Davis, taken by Edward L. Wilson, ca. 1885.

Drawing of Jefferson Davis imprisoned in a casemate at Fortress Monroe, Virginia, following his capture.

Civilians attending the victorious Union troops parading on Pennsylvania Avenue, Washington, DC, in May 1865. Note the completed dome of the U.S. Capitol Building in the background. Photograph by Mathew B. Brady.

THE HUMAN COST OF WAR

After the Civil War, there was a concerted effort to determine the number of Americans killed in this conflict. The number was nearly 620,000. Recently, however, others have looked more closely at the records from the war, and compared these with census records, and determined that perhaps 750,000, or possibly more were killed. As noted at the beginning of this volume, either number is stunning, for one would have to add together the number killed in all wars from the Revolutionary War through most of Vietnam to reach 620,000, and to reach 750,000, even with the Gulf War, Iraq, and Afghanistan, we are not close to that number.

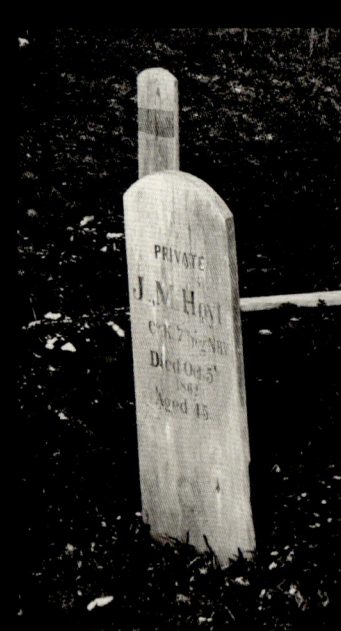

Single gravestone, Savannah, Georgia.

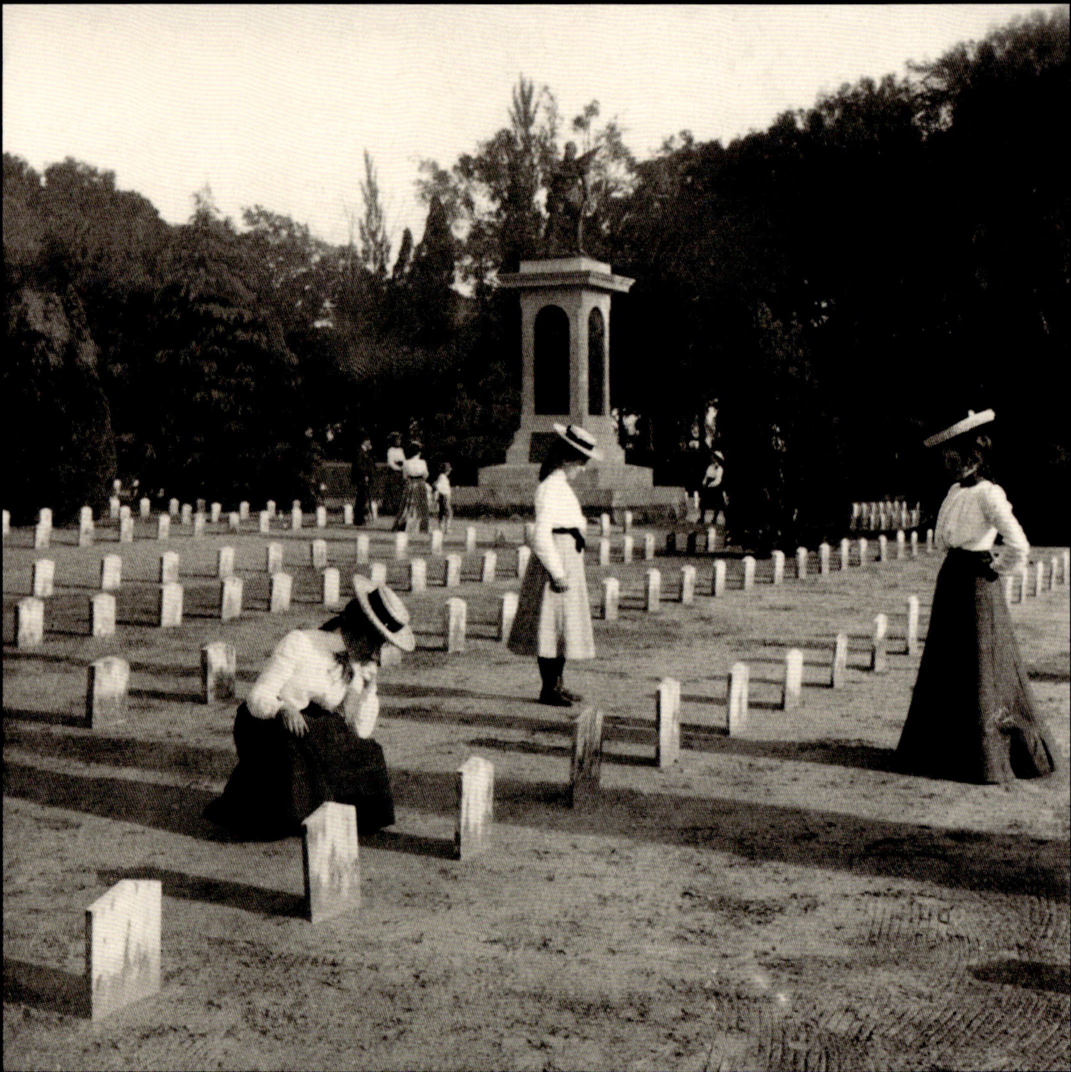

Women mourning the loss of their husbands, brothers, or fathers. Charleston, South Carolina.

One of the many Civil War cemeteries—constant reminders of America's greatest conflict. Grave of Frank L. Smith, a sergeant of the Union from Connecticut. Drewry's Bluff, Virginia.

SOLDIERS' LIFE

RIGHT

Confederate winter quarters at Manassas, Virginia, 1862.

BOTTOM LEFT

Union soldiers writing letters home. The man in the foreground is sewing his clothes.

BOTTOM RIGHT

Interior of an officer's tent. The accommodation of officers was considerably better than that of ordinary soldiers (National Archives Photo Collection).

When not fighting, soldiers spent a lot of their time drilling, marching, setting up encampments, or building field fortifications. Beyond that, they were busy cooking meals, doing laundry, cleaning their weapons, cutting firewood, and writing letters to their loved ones. Soldiers fought boredom and their fear of going into battle by playing cards and dominoes, gambling, horse racing, or singing songs with their comrades around campfires. During the war, camp life was rather primitive. Housing mostly consisted of tents packed with five or six soldiers. The men usually cooked their meals outside on an open fire. During winter, log cabins with fireplaces were used providing insulation from the cold. Early in the war freed slaves joining the Union's armed forces were not permitted to carry a rifle and to fight at the front. As a result, they often worked as cooks or did other similar jobs. Many soldiers' wives accompanied their husbands in camp: they cooked meals, did the laundry, and took care of soldiers' wounds suffered in battle.

Union soldier in camp being accompanied by his wife and children. This harmonious image stands in stark contrast to the cruelties of war.
Note the various everyday items.

THE "BLUE" AND THE "GRAY" CIVIL WAR UNIFORMS

The uniforms used in the Civil War helped distinguish between Union and Confederate soldiers. However, early in the war, uniforms were provided by states, towns, and wealthy individuals. This resulted in a confusing variety of styles and colors on both sides. As a result, almost any variation of the official uniform could be found as officers and ordinary soldiers abandoned some items, adopted others and modified still others. The standard U.S. Army uniform (Union) at the outbreak of the war had acquired its definitive form in the 1858 regulations.

The original Confederate uniforms closely followed the lines of the Union's uniforms.

However, in June of 1861, the Confederate Council issued new regulations for the military. As a result, the German-American artist Nicola Marschall, the designer of the Confederate flag, designed new uniforms. He was influenced by Austrian and French army uniforms of the mid-1800s. Early on Confederate soldiers sometimes wore combinations of uniform pieces, making do with what they could get from captured Union soldiers, or from Union and Confederate dead, or just wear civilian clothing. Eventually, blue became the Union's official color, while the Confederacy chose gray for its uniforms. Both sides used buttons and various types of insignia for identification of rank.

LEFT Private of the infantry, United States Army (U.S. Dept. of War)

RIGHT Private of the infantry, Confederate States Army (U.S. Dept. of War)

The "Gray" (left) and the "Blue" (right)—immortalized in one photo. During one of the numerous engagements of the Peninsular Campaign, Union troops captured Confederate Lieutenant J. B. Washington. Union Lieutenant George A. Custer, a former classmate of Washington, noticed the prisoner of war. As a result, he asked Washington to be photographed with him. Fourteen years later, Custer and all of his men would be killed at the Battle of Little Bighorn against native American tribes, which later would be popularly known as "Custer's Last Stand". Photograph by James F. Gibson.

NEW MEANS OF COMMUNICATION

During the Civil War, several other new means of communication emerged. Photography enabled people to see the war without actually being in combat. In addition, artists sketched pictures of battlefields and significant events. The telegraph allowed the transmission of urgent messages electrically over telegraph wires. This was much faster and more reliable than sending messages by horse-riding messengers. Tall signal towers provided visual communication over short distances by using flags. Newspapers not only took news of the war to other parts of the country, but also brought news from home to the soldiers fighting at the front.

Telegraph wires could easily be disconnected (National Archives Photo Collection).

TOP Front page of *The New York Times,* Monday, April 10, 1865, announcing General Lee's surrender.

LEFT Union telegraph station with two operators.

A group of photographers and soldiers resting in front of a signal tower near Bermuda Hundred, Virginia. Note the plate in the photograph's center, probably belonging to a camera.

EARLY AERIAL WARFARE

Balloons provided humans the first available method of elevating themselves well over the battlefield in order to obtain the proverbial "bird's-eye view." They were used as an early mechanism of aerial reconnaissance—for example troop strengths or movements—and proved their value in the preparation of accurate battlefield maps. During the Civil War, the Union as well as the Confederacy made use of balloons. Professor Thaddeus S. C. Lowe was the chief aeronaut of the Union Army Balloon Corps. He also used balloons to direct artillery fire from an unseen location onto a Confederate encampment.

TOP Professor Thaddeus S. C. Lowe, the father of military aerial reconnaissance in the United States.

LEFT The Union's balloon "Intrepid" being cross-inflated from another balloon.

Professor Lowe ascending to observe the Battle of Seven Pines (Fair Oaks) from his balloon "Intrepid" near Chickahominy, Virginia, during the Peninsular Campaign.

CARING FOR THE WOUNDED

For every soldier killed in combat, two died of illness or disease. Bad drinking water, poor food, and poor clothing, as well as mosquitoes, were major causes of deteriorating health. As a result, tens of thousands of wounded and sick soldiers had to be cared for under wartime conditions. During the Civil War, however, most people in hospitals—including doctors and nurses—were not aware of the need of washing their hands in order to prevent deadly infections.

RIGHT Wounded soldiers with crutches recovering in a hospital. Note the nurse at right.

BOTTOM Medical treatment in a field hospital. The doctor is probably preparing the amputation of an arm.

Consequently, many injured soldiers fell victim to infections, rather than dying from their wounds suffered in combat. Medicine of the 1860s was also relatively primitive and often in short supply. In most cases, the only way of treating a broken arm or leg was either a complete or partial amputation. During the war, various buildings, churches, barns, tents, or wagons near a battlefield were used as hospitals, leaving much to be desired with regards to care and hygiene.

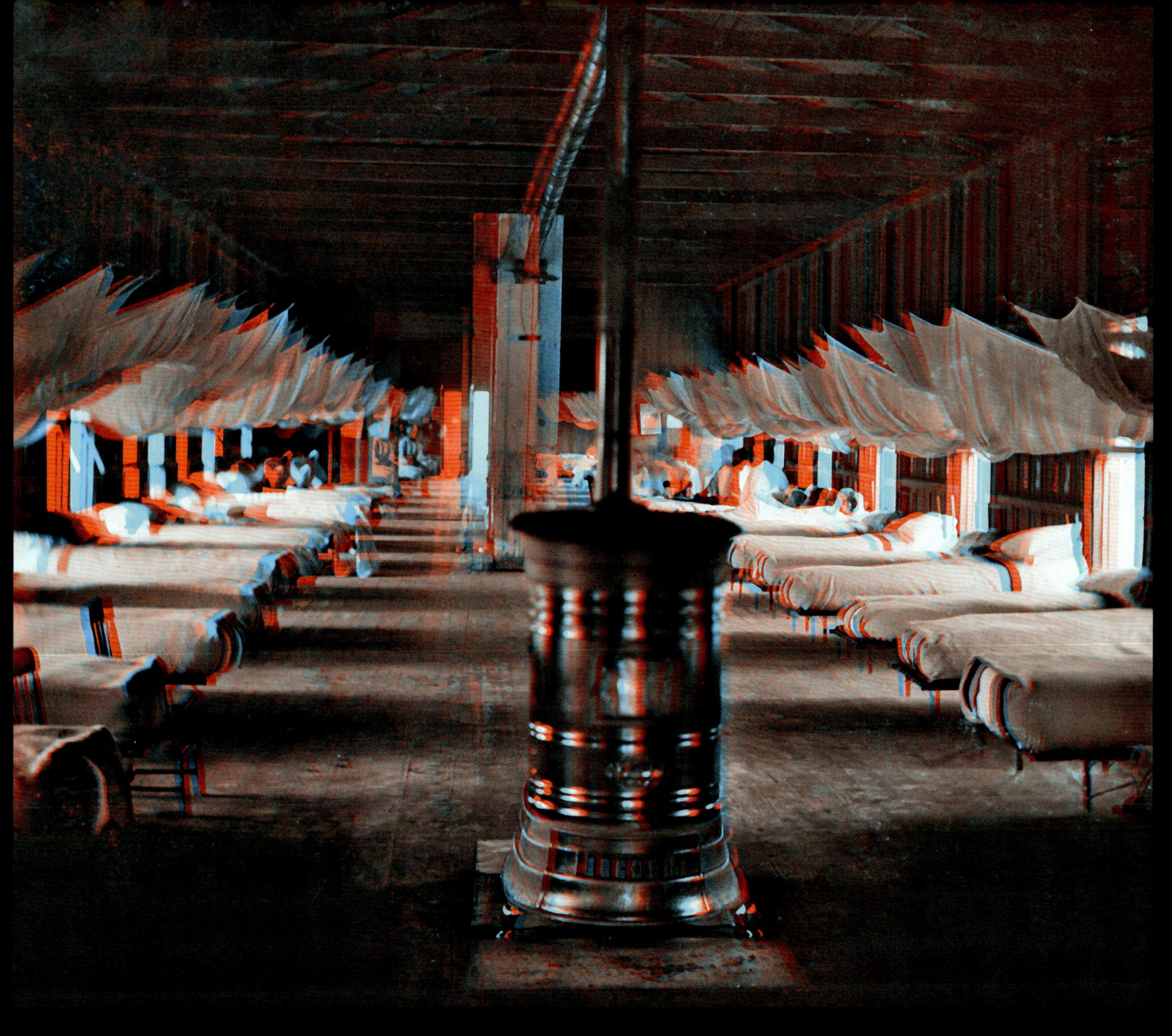

Interior of Harewood Hospital, Washington, DC. Note the mosquito nets over the beds and the stove in the foreground.

During the war, transportation still consisted largely of marching and horseback riding. Horses and wagons were used for moving arms, equipment, and supplies. Ships and trains allowed the transportation of large numbers of troops and heavy materials, such as cannons, over long distances.

Railroads in particular played a significant role in moving men and weapons. This included powerful guns mounted on railroad wagons. As a result, both sides built railroads and bridges, and tried to protect them from destruction by the enemy.

LEFT Army wagon of the Union at the railroad depot, Atlanta, Georgia.
RIGHT Locomotives at the U.S. Military Railroad at City Point, Virginia.

Front side of railroad gun.

Men repairing single-track railroad near Murfreesboro, Tennessee. Because of their strategical role, railroad tracks were often blown up in order to delay the enemy's transportation of troops and supplies.

The Civil War split families and friends, thus leading to the well-known phrase "brother against brother." As men left home to fight the war, women often had to fill their place. They worked as school teachers, clerks, factory workers, and nurses in hospitals. During the war, the Union recruited about 2,500,000 men, while the Confederacy counted about 1,250,000 soldiers—a significant part of the overall population. As a result, many families were left with only mothers and daughters to run the household and to feed the family. As the war progressed, Union troops began to feed themselves off the land they occupied during their advance in the South. Moreover, they destroyed public buildings, railroads, bridges, factories, and other structures taking the war directly to the civilian population of the Confederacy. As a result, the South would suffer enormous shortages in food and other everyday items until the end of the war.

Lithograph of Union soldier dreaming of his welcome home by his wife and child.

Women going to receive government rations in Union-occupied Richmond, Virginia, 1865. Note the women's disrespectful behavior towards the Union officer.

Family posing in front of house, Cedar Mountain, Virginia.

VETERANS OF WAR

After the end of the Civil War, former soldiers from both sides began organizing themselves in organizations such as the "Grand Army of the Republic" (Union) or the "United Confederate Veterans" (Confederacy). In 1913, for the 50th anniversary of the Battle of Gettysburg, some 53,000 veterans from both sides met at the Gettysburg Battlefield. President Woodrow Wilson's reunion address summarized the spirit:

"We have found one another again as brothers and comrades in arms, enemies no longer, generous friends rather, our battles long past, the quarrel forgotten— except that we shall not forget the splendid valor."

The last Gettysburg reunion took place in 1938 commemorating the 75th anniversary of the battle. This event was attended by about 1,900 veterans with an average age of 94. President Franklin D. Roosevelt's reunion address preceded the unveiling of the Eternal Light Peace Memorial. In 1956, former Union soldier Albert H. Woolson—the last confirmed American Civil War veteran on either side—passed away at the age of 108.

Veterans of the Confederacy during the reunion at Gettysburg in 1913.

Veterans from the Confederacy (left) and Union (right) shaking hands during the reunion at Gettysburg in 1913.

Photograph of John L. Burns (1793–1872), a veteran of the War of 1812. He became a 70-year-old combatant at Gettysburg in 1863 fighting for the Union. During the battle, he was wounded, but recovered to become a national hero. Note the rifle in the right corner.

REMEMBERING THE CIVIL WAR

April 2011 marked the 150th anniversary of the start of the American Civil War (1861–1865). At this occasion, Dr. Robert K. Sutton, the Chief Historian of the National Park Service since 2007, shared his thoughts on this epic conflict and its meaning today. As the Chief Historian, he "provides guidance and direction to the national parks as well as to the American people on the importance of verifying historical events and interpreting America's historic places." Before being appointed to this office, Dr. Sutton was Superintendent of the Manassas National Battlefield Park in Virginia.

How did people commemorate the Civil War during its 25th and 50th anniversaries?

Dr. Sutton: I really haven't found much on how the war was commemorated at the 25th anniversary. The process of reconciliation was beginning to bring soldiers from both sides together, and they were beginning to lobby Congress to set aside many of the major battlefields as sacred places. In 1889, the movement gathered steam as the former commanders from both sides joined about 12,000 former soldiers and others at Chickamauga Battlefield for speeches and a giant barbecue, to commemorate the battle, and to push for the creation of a military park. The park was established a year later.

Dr. Robert K. Sutton posing with a Civil War cannon (Photo: Collection Dr. Robert Sutton).

By the 50th anniversary, the reconciliation process was in full swing. In July of 1913, survivors of the Battle of Gettysburg were part of a crowd of 50,000 who gathered at the battlefield. In the now famous picture and moving film, survivors of Pickett's Charge tottered up and shook hands over the stone wall that was there in 1863. President Woodrow Wilson, the first southern President elected after the war, spoke, and touted the fact that both sides had fully reconciled, and that the war could be considered "a quarrel forgotten." What he didn't mention, and what was completely lost in all of the commemorations, was that the war ended slavery, and that some 200,000 African American soldiers and sailors fought in the war. No one wanted to deal with the Jim Crow laws and practices that had reduced African Americans to second-class citizenship at the time.

How does the commemoration for the 150th anniversary differ from the 100th anniversary?

Dr. Sutton: The 100th anniversary was interesting. Congress created a Centennial Commission that was charged with leading the commemoration of the war. Retired General Ulysses S. Grant III was named chairman of the commission, and its purpose was to increase American patriotism during the Cold War and to encourage tourism to Civil War battlefields and commemorative events. The commission got off to a rocky start. Its first meeting was to be held in Charleston, South Carolina, but one of the commission members, an African American woman, was denied a reservation in a Charleston hotel. This ignited a furor even before the commission was able to do its business. The meeting was moved to the Charleston Naval Yard. Many southerners viewed the centennial as an opportunity to dull the effects and impacts of the Civil Rights Movement that was gathering steam throughout the South.

Eventually, the Kennedy Administration tried to change the course of the centennial by replacing Grant, who resigned for family reasons, with noted historian Allan Nevins and a young professor from Virginia Tech, James (Bud) Robertson. Nevins and Robertson tried to shift the focus to a more thoughtful, history based, commemoration, but the centennial lost steam, especially in the South.

Photograph of the *March on Washington,* August 28, 1963, showing civil rights and union leaders, including Martin Luther King, Jr. (National Archives).

Interestingly, the best source on the centennial is a book written by a British historian, Robert Cook, titled *Troubled Commemoration.*

For various reasons, Congress did not establish a commission to commemorate the 150th anniversary, so there is no national leadership for the commemoration. Congress also has not appropriated any money for the sesquicentennial. A number of states have established commissions, and some, like Virginia, are doing an outstanding job of commemorating the war. The National Park Service, with its 20 major battlefields and over 75 parks associated with the war, has become the de facto national organization coordinating the 150th.

Our main focus, which has been ongoing for several years, is to expand the interpretation of the Civil War, to go beyond "who shot whom, how, when and where." We believe it is important to talk about the causes, and to emphasize that slavery was the principal cause of the war. We talk more about the common soldiers, their views of the war, and its impact on them. We focus on families. What was it like for the families of the more than 600,000 fathers and sons who did not return home? What was it like for the many more who returned with missing limbs or who suffered from post traumatic shock syndrome, which no one understood at that time? We are also talking about what it was like for women, who had to take on new roles to feed their families, to take care of their households, and/ or to try to maintain the institution of slavery on southern plantations. We also want to focus on the aftermath of the war, the Reconstruction and post-Reconstruction eras.

What is the most important thing people should know about the Civil War?

Dr. Sutton: Slavery was the principal cause of the war. Without the institution of slavery, and the fact that 4,000,000 humans were enslaved, I can't imagine that the war would have ever happened. The war ended the institution of slavery in the United States forever. Enslaved individuals took a very active part in ending the institution, by escaping, by joining the Union war effort, and by keeping constant pressure on the military, Congress, and President Lincoln to make the end of slavery a war aim.

What do you think was the most interesting event associated with the war and why?

Dr. Sutton: This is a tough one, because there are so many truly interesting events. But, in my mind, the most interesting event was the escape of Robert Smalls in Charleston, South Carolina Harbor in May of 1862. Smalls was an enslaved man who was the wheelman (actually pilot) on the Confederate harbor steamer *Planter.* The *Planter* was a converted cotton steamer used to deliver arms and supplies to the Confederate forts in the harbor. Smalls and the enslaved crew plotted for weeks to commandeer the ship, pick up their families, sail through the harbor, and surrender the ship to the Union naval blockade just outside the harbor entrance. They pulled it off on the night of May 12th–13th, when the white crew went ashore for the night. They fired up the boilers, sailed over to another wharf where they picked up their families and several other enslaved men, and sailed through the harbor, giving the proper signals to all of the forts.

Smalls later piloted several Union vessels during the war, including the *Planter* of which he became the captain. He later served several terms in the United States House of Representatives and was a major political figure in South Carolina. He purchased the house in Beaufort, South Carolina that had belonged to his former master—the house and property where he was born. The house is currently a National Historic Landmark and it stands as a memorial to this truly amazing man.

Of all sites associated with the Civil War, which do you think is the most interesting to see and why?

Dr. Sutton: Again, this is a tough one. I would have to say that Fort (or sometimes referred to as Fortress) Monroe, near the mouth of Chesapeake Bay, is the most interesting. First of all, it is one of our newest national parks. Built shortly after the War of 1812, it was the largest masonry fort in the United States. It was in continuous military use until closed in 2011. So, the history itself is fascinating. The Union held onto Fort Monroe through the Civil War as a vital piece in the Union blockade of Southern ports. Fort Monroe rises to my most interesting site because on May 23, 1861, only six weeks after the firing on Fort Sumter, three enslaved men who were forced to work on a Confederate fortification under construction and to fire on Fortress Monroe, snuck away from their camp, commandeered a boat, sailed it across the harbor, and presented themselves to General Benjamin Butler, the commander at Fortress Monroe.

Butler, who was a lawyer in civilian life, invoked the legal principle that the three men were property of the enemy, and thus contraband of war. Soon, word spread among the networks of enslaved people and a flood tide of others left Confederate work sites and plantations and fled to Union lines. Enslaved people did not wait to see if the end of slavery would become a Union war aim. Early on, starting at Fort Monroe, they seized the opportunity to end slavery by escaping bondage on their own initiative.

Why are Americans, and even non-Americans, so fascinated by this war above all others?

Dr. Sutton: I wish there was a simple answer to this question! If there is, I have never found it. Many are fascinated with the military history. At our National Park Service Civil War battlefields, visitors still flock to our tours and many can never get enough of the battles, tactics, commanders, etc. People are interested in global military history—how the war shifted from a limited war to a hard war. They are fascinated with Sherman's March to the Sea in Georgia and Sheridan's march through the Shenandoah Valley.

Then, there are particular interests. Once I checked on the number of books currently in print on the telegraph in the Civil War. I quit counting at 35. The number of reenactors has increased dramatically over the past 20 to 30 years, and while their interests vary, many really want to understand the war by trying to relive it. There is an intellectual curiosity with the war. Americans wonder how the "land of the free" could not only condone slavery, but how they fought this tragic, bloody war over the institution. Of course, there are still many who subscribe to the "Lost Cause" view, that the war really had nothing to do with slavery, but was fought over the issue of states' rights or state sovereignty, economics, etc.

I am particularly fascinated with how people in other countries have such a fascination with our Civil War. It is almost an obsession with Australians and Canadians. I think they view the war as something that could have happened to them, but didn't, so they look at it vicariously as something they were able to avoid.

This interview was conducted by The Ultimate History Project, an online web Journal, which can be read at www.ultimatehistoryproject.com.